THE BALUSTERS

Broadway Edition

Other Books by David Lindsay-Abaire Published by TCG

Kimberly Akimbo (music by Jeanine Tesori)

Ripcord

Good People

Rabbit Hole

PRAISE FOR *THE BALUSTERS*

"A terrifically chaotic new comedy from David Lindsay-Abaire."

—Melissa Rose Bernardo, *New York Stage Review*

"*The Balusters* is thrilling to watch from start to finish, a sort of respectable cage match with a typed agenda and tea served on family china. Welcome to the liberal thunderdome."

—Christian Lewis, *New York Theatre Guide*

"A prime example of when art imitates life."

—Mekishana Pierre, *Entertainment Weekly*

"Lindsay-Abaire's collection of oddballs is a jury duty lineup of eccentric personalities that, the more they spar, the louder we laugh . . . Line by line and moment by moment, *The Balusters* is an engrossing and enjoyable watch, fueled by Lindsay-Abaire's impolite humor."

—Johnny Oleksinski, *New York Post*

"*The Balusters* is hilarious, skewering not only neighborhood associations but also identity politics while maintaining compassion for all its characters. Too bad real HOA meetings can't be this fun."

—Rachel Graham, *TheaterMania*

"A razor-sharp show loaded with non-stop laugh-out-loud one-liners, politically incorrect accusations and affronts, and sidesplitting sight gags . . . *The Balusters* delivers the message loud (sometimes extremely so) and clear, by being riotously satirical, not preachy. It will keep you laughing and leave you thinking about what it truly means to be a good, albeit imperfect, person."

—Deb Miller, *DC Theater Arts*

"Who ever thought discussions over a stop sign could generate so many sparks of lightning-fresh humor? And as would be expected from a playwright of his caliber, Lindsay-Abaire gets in some keen-eyed commentary on where we are at this quarter mark of the twenty-first century."

—Ron Fassler, *Theater Pizzazz*

"If any playwright could be described as the American Alan Ayckbourn—and that is a high compliment, that triple A—it's David Lindsay-Abaire . . . *The Balusters* is a satirical comedy of manners where the manners gradually dissipate, only to be replaced by anger, fear, and resentment. As the days and months go by, small digs turn to larger insults, which in turn reveal grievances long-standing and new. The internecine battles would all be painful to witness if they weren't so damn funny."

—Randall David Cook, *The Recs*

"This is comedy with teeth, where civility is a costume and hypocrisy is the true language spoken . . . Visually and structurally, *The Balusters* functions as a true ensemble piece, with each actor contributing to Lindsay-Abaire's layered dissection of privilege and perception."

—Suzanna Bowling, *Times Square Chronicles*

THE BALUSTERS

Broadway Edition

DAVID LINDSAY-ABAIRE

THEATRE COMMUNICATIONS GROUP
NEW YORK
2026

The Balusters (Broadway Edition) is published by
Theatre Communications Group, Inc., 520 Eighth Avenue, 20th Floor,
Suite 2000, New York, NY 10018-4156

TCG books are exclusively distributed to the book trade by Consortium Book Sales and Distribution.

Library of Congress Control Number: 2026937539
ISBN 978-1-63670-264-3 (paperback) / 978-1-63670-269-8 (ebook)
A catalog record for this book is available from the Library of Congress.

www.tcg.org
Follow us on Instagram @tcg_gram

Book design and composition by Lisa Govan
Cover design by Lisa Govan
Cover illustration by Robert Neubecker for Serino Coyne,
used by permission of Manhattan Theatre Club

Broadway Edition, April 2026

ACKNOWLEDGMENTS

First and foremost, I need to thank everyone at Manhattan Theatre Club for their unwavering support and dedication to developing new American plays, most especially Lynne Meadow, who has given me an artistic home since 1999 when she first produced my play *Fuddy Meers*. *The Balusters* marks our seventh collaboration, and I will always be in her debt. In addition to Lynne, I need to thank the new Artistic Director, Nicki Hunter, whose sharp eye and steady hand helped steer this play to the stage. Additional thanks to Jeff Brancato, David Caparelliotis (who has helped cast every one of my plays at MTC), Robert Carroll, Steven Dalton, Malaika Fernandes, Kelly Gillespie, Chris Jennings, Scott Kaplan, Amy Gilkes Loe, Debra Waxman-Pilla, and everyone else on staff.

I'm also indebted to the amazing cast, crew, and designers of the Broadway production of this play, starting with our fearless leader, Kenny Leon, whose pitch-perfect direction brought the play to life, as well as Ioana Alfonso, Carissa Barry-Moilanen, Janette Braggs, Marylouise Burke, Melody Butiu, Tony Carlin, Kayli Carter, Ricardo Chavira, Ka-Ling

Cheung, Carl Clemons-Hopkins, Margaret Colin, Michael Esper, Sophie Hayden, Deborah Hecht, Stacey Highsmith, Allen Lee Hughes, Mike Iveson, J. Jared Janas, Alvin Keith, Grace Keith, Derek McLane, Maria-Christina Oliveras, Lena Pepe, Tripp Phillips, Jaadyn Rogers, Anika Noni Rose, Thomas Schall, Dan Moses Schreier, Emilio Sosa, Richard Thomas, Luis Vega, Chloe Yasmine, and Jeena Yi.

Special thanks also need to go to several friends and colleagues who contributed their invaluable insight, talent, and support during the development of *The Balusters*: Ali Ahn, Tanya Barfield, Eboni Booth, Christopher Fitzgerald, Melissa Jane Gibson, Daniel Goldfarb, Renée Elise Goldsberry, Karen Hartman, Mia Katigbak, Carlos Korten, Gerri Korten, Krista Knight, T.R. Knight, Joe Kraemer, Deborah Zoe Laufer, Lauren Patten, Siena Rafter, David Stone, Jessica Stone, JD Taylor, Jeanine Tesori, Lucy Thurber, Michael Benjamin Washington, Krista Williams, Beau Willimon, Sheri Wilner, and David Zayas.

I'm especially thankful to my agent extraordinaire, John Buzzetti, whose not-so-gentle nudging encouraged me to finish this play when I wasn't sure I could.

I'd be remiss if I didn't also thank my Prospect Park South neighbors, both past and present. That said, any resemblance to actual persons, events, or neighborhood dustups is purely coincidental, I swear.

But above all, I want to thank my family: my sons, Nicholas and Cooper, and my wife, Chris, whose stories from the front line of a neighborhood board proved irresistible to the scavenger-writer she happens to be married to. This play, like most every good thing in my life, wouldn't exist without her.

THE BALUSTERS

Broadway Edition

PRODUCTION HISTORY

The Balusters had its world premiere on Broadway at the Manhattan Theatre Club (Nicki Hunter, Artistic Director; Chris Jennings, Executive Director; and Lynne Meadow, Artistic Advisor) at the Samuel J. Friedman Theatre. The first performance was on March 31, 2026. It was directed by Kenny Leon. The scenic design was by Derek McLane, the costume design was by Emilio Sosa, the lighting design was by Allen Lee Hughes, the sound design and original music was by Dan Moses Schreier, the hair, wig, and makeup design was by J. Jared Janas, the fight direction was by Thomas Schall, the vocal coach was Deborah Hecht, the movement and associate director was Ioana Alfonso, casting was by Caparelliotis Casting/ Kelly Gillespie, and the production stage manager was Tripp Phillips. The cast was:

PENNY BUELL	Marylouise Burke
WILLOW GIBBONS	Kayli Carter
ISAAC ROSARIO	Ricardo Chavira
BROOKS DUNCAN	Carl Clemons-Hopkins
RUTH ACKERMAN	Margaret Colin
ALAN KIRBY	Michael Esper
LUZ BACCAY	Maria-Christina Oliveras
KYRA MARSHALL	Anika Noni Rose

ELLIOT EMERSON	Richard Thomas
MELISSA HAN	Jeena Yi

The Balusters was commissioned by Manhattan Theatre Club through the Bank of America New Play Commissioning Program and is a recipient of an Edgerton Foundation New Play Award.

PLACE

The play is set in Vernon Point, a tree-lined, landmarked enclave of an East Coast city. The neighborhood, with its front lawns, large Victorian houses, and expansive porches, has the vibe of a wealthy suburb, but if you walk a few blocks, just beyond the boundaries of the historic district, you'll find apartment buildings, discount stores, and housing projects.

The set is the interior of one of the impressive Victorian homes, built in 1905. Most of the stage is taken up by the ample front parlor. There's a tasteful couch, a secretary desk, and several accent chairs—enough seating for at least nine people. There are end tables, probably some artwork (by African American artists), and a fireplace upstage center with family photos arranged on the mantel. There's also at least one window upstage right that looks out onto a wraparound porch, and through which, when the shades are up, we can see visitors as they approach the front door.

Also upstage right, stage left of the window, is a wide-open double doorway, and beyond the doorway is the foyer of the house.

In the foyer, the front door is stage right. We'll see people enter and even have small scenes here. Also in the foyer, we may be able to see a set of stairs that lead up to the rest of the house. A hall heads off stage left from the foyer. Characters may go down that hall to get to the coat closet, as well as the kitchen beyond it.

Back to the front parlor—upstage left we can also see at least part of a dining room. In some scenes, refreshments, wine, cheese, and crackers will be arranged on the dining room table and sideboard. Characters may walk into the dining room but still be seen by the audience. Also in the dining room is a door upstage left that leads to the pass-through butler's pantry and the kitchen beyond it. In between the parlor and the dining room is a pair of pocket doors, which will be closed in some scenes (blocking the audience's view of the dining room).

Although this house was built in 1905, the furniture and decor shouldn't feel like musty museum pieces. The owners are tasteful people who have respect for the history of their home but still want to live in the present. If there's a Victrola somewhere, there might also be some chairs from Restoration Hardware. Most everything should feel like it belongs in these rooms and to this specific family.

CHARACTERS

KYRA MARSHALL: African American, forties. Kyra is new to the neighborhood and even newer to the board of the Neighborhood Association. She's gracious, warm, and eager to fit in. But she sometimes has trouble biting her tongue, which has gotten her into trouble in the past. Kyra is sharp, savvy, and like all of us, has her blind spots.

LUZ BACCAY: Filipino, fifties. Luz is Kyra's new housekeeper. She's worked for families in the neighborhood for decades and lived just outside its borders for just as long. She's genial and very comfortable in these houses. She clocks pretty much everything but usually knows what to keep to herself. If she sometimes lets a zinger slip, it's said in a way that you're not sure it's meant to be a zinger.

MELISSA HAN: Asian American, forties. Vice president of the Neighborhood Association. Melissa has lived in Vernon Point for a decade and has most of her neighbors figured out. She's a lawyer, quick-witted, and enjoys stirring the pot. She may secretly covet Elliot's gavel and position on the board.

PENNY BUELL: White, seventies. Secretary of the Neighborhood Association. One of the "old timers" in the group, she's a widow who has worked for years answering the phones at

Elliot's real estate office. Penny is usually kind and good-natured and, though she's not as sharp as she once was, she's still sharper than most people think.

RUTH ACKERMAN: White, seventies. Treasurer of the Neighborhood Association. Ruth is another Vernon Point stalwart. She's outspoken, prickly, and wry. She's self-aware and winning, which means she often gets away with saying things that no one else can. She's also kinder than she pretends to be.

ISAAC ROSARIO: Latino, fifties. He's a chummy, salt of the earth guy with some conservative leanings. Isaac doesn't come from money (which he's proud of), but he has it now (which he's also proud of). He's authentic and he admires that quality in others. He has no patience for whatever he considers bullshit.

BROOKS DUNCAN: African American, forties. Brooks is a travel writer and a married guy with a kid. He's mostly amiable, but sometimes these people try his nerves. He's hopeful about the new energy Kyra might bring to the group. Brooks enjoys neighborhood intrigue, so long as it doesn't involve him. He and his husband might be having some problems.

ALAN KIRBY: White, fifties. Alan is friendly and genuine and has always prided himself on being a well-intentioned, nice guy, which is why he's so unnerved when anyone gets offended by something he's said. Alan is also not the most assertive person, which can work against him with this particular crowd.

WILLOW GIBBONS: White, thirties. Willow grew up here. She inherited her father's house as well as his spot on the board. She's ultraliberal and has only ever worked for nonprofits. Her views are earnest and noble, which can be annoying to some people. She tries hard not to be strident, but she doesn't always succeed.

ELLIOT EMERSON: White, seventies. President of the Neighborhood Association. He grew up in Vernon Point and considers himself its protector, clinging to its history and traditions. He's a realtor and has sold most of the houses in the neighborhood. He's eminently likable—an affable and reasonable guy (so long as no one challenges his opinions or advocates for change).

NOTE

A slash (/) in the dialogue indicates the start of the next spoken line.

Brackets [ ] indicate words that are thought but not spoken aloud.

SCENE I

April Meeting
Vernon Point Neighborhood Association

The parlor of a Victorian home. Dusk. The shades are up. Kyra Marshall, forties, African American, arranges chairs for a meeting. On the coffee table are bowls of cashews and grapes. There is a stocked drink cart stage right. Upstage left is a dining room with light fare, snacks, plates, wine glasses, etc. Off of the dining room is a door that leads to the kitchen via a butler's pantry. There's a small stack of fancy dessert plates on a side table which Kyra moves to the coffee table. She then reconsiders and moves the plates back to where they were.

Luz Baccay, fifties, Filipino, enters from the dining room with a small basket.

LUZ

I put the crackers in a basket. Unless you want them *around* the cheese. *(Shows her the basket)*

KYRA

No, I like the crackers separate. It's less messy.

LUZ

And did you decide about the cocktails?

KYRA

Do you know if Ken had cocktails when *he* hosted?

LUZ

Oh yes. Too many in fact. Which is why he no longer hosts.

KYRA

Then let's just stick with the wine.

(Luz puts the crackers in the dining room. She adjusts things on the table.

Sound of screeching tires and car horns outside. Kyra looks to a window, annoyed.)

You see what I'm saying about that intersection? Last week there was an actual *crash*. Two in the morning—*BOOM*! Woke us all up out of a dead sleep. *(Back to Luz)* You'd think Elliot would've said something when he showed us the house, "Just FYI—the corner's a problem."

LUZ

It's because they installed that traffic light up on Haskell. Now the cars cut over here and fly down Palmer to avoid the light.

KYRA

Oh. I didn't realize that light was *new*.

LUZ

You should bring it up. At the meeting.

KYRA

Huh. Maybe. Probably not tonight though. First impressions. I don't want to seem too pushy. *(Spots someone through the window)* There's Melissa.

(Doorbell. Kyra heads to the front door. She lets in Melissa Han, forties, Asian American.)

MELISSA	KYRA
Heeeey-eeeey.	Hey, you. Get in here.

MELISSA

Did you hear those cars? Some jackass just came flying down / Palmer.

KYRA

No, I know. They make me crazy. *(Takes her jacket)* Oo, I like this outfit.

MELISSA

Thank you. Bailey said it was giving Kelly McGillis vibes, but I don't even know what that means.

(Kyra heads down the hall to the coat closet as Melissa steps into the parlor. She eats some cashews.)

This looks great. You sure you're ready for these people?

KYRA

(Off) Should I be worried?

MELISSA

Oh yeah, you should definitely be worried. *(Spots Luz in the dining room)* Oh, hi. Sorry, I didn't see you. I was busy stealing cashews.

LUZ

(Steps into the parlor) That's why they're there.

MELISSA

I'm Melissa. I live a couple blocks over. And I work with Leon actually. *(To Kyra as she reenters behind her)* She's adorable. *(Back to Luz)* You're adorable. I hope that's okay to say. I could've picked you out of a lineup. You look so much like Leon.

KYRA

What are you talking about?

MELISSA

Your mother-in-law. The family resemblance is / like—

KYRA

Luz isn't my mother-in-law.

MELISSA

Oh. Oh my god. I just assumed— Leon said his mom was gonna visit—

KYRA

At Easter. She's coming when the girls are on break.

LUZ

I'm Luz. I'm the housekeeper.

KYRA

You don't need to say / housekeeper.

MELISSA

I am so sorry. I cut out caffeine this week so I'm not firing on all cylinders.

KYRA

You think she looks like Leon?

MELISSA

I mean . . . No, I know, I'm the worst. Can we rewind please? *(A fresh start)* Hi, I'm Melissa. It's nice to meet you.

LUZ

We've met before. A few times actually.

MELISSA

Oh god, this just gets worse / and worse.

KYRA

(Laughs) You're really putting your foot in it.

LUZ

I worked for the Emersons.

MELISSA

Yes! Of *course*! *That's* why you look familiar! Elliot's house. The holiday parties.

LUZ

Maybe it's because I'm not wearing the uniform. The Emersons *liked* the uniform, but Mrs. Marshall prefers I not wear it.

KYRA

I just want you to be comfortable.

LUZ

I'm comfortable either way. *(Silence, then to Melissa)* I'm gonna get you some wine. I remember you prefer red, yes?

MELISSA

Well now you're just rubbing it in. But yes, red please.

(Luz heads into the dining room.)

What is wrong with me? I totally pulled a Penny.

KYRA

How do you mean?

MELISSA

Penny always confuses me with the *other* Melissa in the neighborhood.

KYRA

Melissa *Kahn*? She's *Indian*.

MELISSA

Pakistani, but yeah. Penny gets us mixed up.

KYRA

(Laughing) Oh, no.

MELISSA

And the best part? She always asks after *Bernie*—the other Melissa's husband. It's been going on so long that I can't even correct her now. *(Eats another cashew)* You know she'll be here tonight, right? You'll get to see her in action.

(Luz brings Melissa her wine.)

Thank you, Luz. And again, I'm sorry. I think I have that thing where you can't remember certain . . .

LUZ

Alzheimer's?

MELISSA

No, not Alzheimer's. Jesus, I hope I don't have *Alzheimer's*.

KYRA

Face blindness.

MELISSA

Face blindness, thank you. I do it all the time. It's not just you.

LUZ

Okay.

(A moment. Luz heads off.)

MELISSA

She hates me. *(Regards Kyra)* Are you nervous? You seem nervous.

KYRA

(Adjusts a chair) I wasn't, but Leon was like, "Don't say too much tonight, we want to fit in with these people. Don't do what you did in Baltimore."

MELISSA

The co-op?

KYRA

He told you?

MELISSA

Why do you think I wanted you on the board?

KYRA

Don't say that. This is supposed to be my do-over. I promised to behave myself tonight.

(Doorbell.)

MELISSA

(Spots Penny out the window) Oh, there's Penny now. Strap yourself in.

(Luz crosses to answer the door. She lets in Penny Buell, seventies, white.)

LUZ

Hello, Mrs. Buell.

PENNY

Oh, hello, Luz. It's always nice to see you. *(Takes off her jacket)* Something's different though. Don't tell me what it is. It's not your hair, I don't think. Have you maybe lost a few pounds?

LUZ

I wish.

PENNY

Well whatever it is, you look terrific.

KYRA

Hello, Penny. / Come on in.

MELISSA

There she is.

PENNY

I'm a little early. I like to scope out the seating options. For my back. *(Realizes)* Oh, I just figured it out! It's the house! That's what's different. You're usually answering *Elliot's* door.

LUZ

That's right. I work for Mrs. Marshall now.

PENNY

Oh, that's wonderful.

(Luz takes Penny's jacket to hang in the closet. Penny steps into the parlor.)

(Whispers) Does Elliot know that you've hired his housekeeper?

KYRA

Um, I'm not sure. Why? Is that a problem?

PENNY

Oh, I don't know, you should talk to Elliot about that.

KYRA

Huh. Okay, that's a little . . . [weird.]

PENNY

Hello, Melissa. It's been a little while. How's your *Bernie*?

MELISSA

(Beat) Bernie's great. He sends his love.

(A tap at the window. Ruth Ackerman, seventies, white, gives a little wave.)

RUTH

Yoo-hoo!

PENNY

Uh-oh. I better plant my flag before Ruth muscles her way in here.

(Penny sets her things on a chair as Kyra lets in Ruth. She's wearing a rabbit fur jacket.)

RUTH

I didn't want to ring the bell if you had dogs.

KYRA

No, no dogs. The girls are allergic.

RUTH

Lucky you. My shih tzu goes nuts whenever the doorbell rings. It makes me want to strangle him. *(Sees Luz approach)* Oh, hello, Luz. I see you're here now. Good for you. *(To Kyra)* We love Luz. *(Steps into the parlor)* There's a crowd right behind me. I tried to goose them along, but they're all admiring your new shingles. The house looks gorgeous by the way.

KYRA

Thanks to Isaac and his crew. I just cut the checks.

RUTH

Well that's the most important part. Hello, Penny. I see you've already grabbed the best chair.

PENNY

Because of my back.

RUTH

I was sure I'd be late. My Lizzy wouldn't get off the phone. She's going through a divorce. I'm trying to be supportive, but this is number three. At this point she's obviously the problem. *(Notices Luz waiting)* I'm going to keep my jacket *on* if you don't mind.

KYRA

If you're chilly, I can turn up the heat.

RUTH

Oh god no, I'm sweating actually, but I want Willow to see this.

MELISSA

(Explains to Kyra) Willow works for PETA.

PENNY

Ruth has always had a thing for rabbit fur.

RUTH

So what? It's not like they're *endangered*. There are always plenty of rabbits. That's kinda their thing. And people *love* this jacket. *(Back to Luz)* Would you like to borrow it, Luz?

LUZ

(Beat) It's not really my style.

(The doorbell rings.)

KYRA

Oh, there they are. You all should grab some food.

(Luz and Kyra go to the door. The others head to the dining room to get snacks.

A small group enters: Alan Kirby, fifties, white; Isaac Rosario, fifties, Latino; Willow Gibbons, early thirties, white; and Brooks Duncan, forties, African American. They shed their jackets over the following.)

ISAAC	BROOKS	ALAN
Ding dong.	The riffraff has arrived.	Hide the silverware.

KYRA

Hey, you all, come on in. Luz can take your jackets.

WILLOW

We were just drooling over your cedar shingles.

KYRA

Compliment Isaac, not me.

ISAAC

No, compliment my crew. I haven't been on a ladder in years. I just point now. "Get up there. Fix this. Hammer that."

ALAN

Big improvement from the aluminum siding.

KYRA

Wasn't that awful?

BROOKS

You should ask Elliot about that siding.

RUTH

(Calls from the dining room) Do not! He's been complaining for forty years. I can't hear it again.

(Most of the newcomers have stepped into the parlor. Alan takes some of the jackets from Luz.)

LUZ

You don't need to do that, Mr. Kirby.

ALAN

I'm happy to help. Just show me where they go.

(They head off to the coat closet.)

KYRA

We're just waiting for Elliot. There's wine and snacks in the dining room. Help yourselves. We made a couple vegan dishes, Willow.

WILLOW

You're nice to think of me.

KYRA

I've *tried* to go meatless, but my primal instincts win out every time.

(Folks head for the dining room. Penny, food in hand, hurries back lest anyone steal her seat.)

Hey, Brooks. How was Iceland?

BROOKS

Amazing. Except Chaz was mad he didn't get to go. He was stuck at home dealing with Luke's stomach bug.

KYRA

Oh, no.

BROOKS

Yeah, I FaceTimed from a thermal spa while he was cleaning up vomit. I felt terrible, but it's my job. What could I do?

KYRA

Maybe not FaceTime from a thermal spa?

BROOKS

Yeah, that's exactly what Chaz said.

(Ruth and Melissa return. Alan enters the dining room from the kitchen.)

MELISSA

Are we gonna see Leon tonight?

KYRA

No, he brought the girls to robotics class.

PENNY

Robotics class?

BROOKS

It's that new place on Sewell. It's for kids.

PENNY

And they build *robots*?

(Brooks heads to the dining room as Willow and Isaac come back with food.)

RUTH

Aren't you going to say anything about my jacket?

WILLOW

I've been trying not to.

RUTH

It's rabbit fur. Don't you wanna touch it?

WILLOW

No, thank you.

RUTH

Come on, give it a pat. It's so soft. Like a bunny.

WILLOW

Like a *dead* bunny, you mean. I'm not gonna pat your jacket.

ISAAC

Hey, Ruth, I stopped outside your house yesterday.

RUTH

Oh yeah? Were you casing the joint?

MELISSA

Ruth, no. You can't say that.

RUTH

What? Why not?

WILLOW

You just asked a Latinx man if he was planning to rob your home.

RUTH

Oh for godsakes, it was a joke. It's one of my lines. I say it to everyone.

PENNY

And it never gets old.

ISAAC

I was more bothered that you called me Latinx.

PENNY

Sounds like a superhero.

ISAAC

Sounds like retro woke bullshit, you mean.

WILLOW	MELISSA	KYRA
Come on, Isaac.	Here we go.	Uh-oh.

ISAAC

You know who I've never heard use that word? *Latin* people.

PENNY

So I *shouldn't* call you Latinx?

ISAAC

No, for *me* Latino is fine.

PENNY

Huh. May I also call you Hispanic?

ISAAC

Sure, you can call me Hispanic.

PENNY

And what about Spanish?

ISAAC

I'm not from Spain, so no, not Spanish.

PENNY

Interesting.

BROOKS

(Returns from the dining room) It's not too late, Kyra. You can still escape.

RUTH

So why'd you stop at my house?

ISAAC

I was admiring your crocuses. Vicky's busy with her patients so she assigned me the garden. I've been trying to learn about flowers, but I think I'm too old.

MELISSA

No, you're just a late bloomer.

PENNY

(Chuckles) "Late bloomer."

RUTH

Well you can't go wrong with crocuses. They pop up early and announce the spring. *(Offers Willow her jacket sleeve) Now* do you wanna touch my bunny?

WILLOW

Honestly Ruth, I can't tell if you're harassing me or flirting.

RUTH

Ha! If I had a *nickel . . . (To Luz as she reenters)* Okay Luz, you can take the jacket. I'm about to faint.

(Luz exits with the jacket. Doorbell. Kyra goes to get it as Alan sits beside Penny.)

ALAN

How are your headaches, Penny?

PENNY

Depends on the weather. *(Explains to Melissa)* I've recently developed barometric migraines. They're debilitating. That storm last week just about killed me.

MELISSA

Bummer.

(Kyra lets in Elliot Emerson, seventies, white. He carries a leather satchel.)

ELLIOT

Hi, sorry, I was just printing out the agendas. Am I the last?

KYRA

It's fine, everyone just got here.

ALAN

(Announces to the others) The president has *arrived*!

(Everyone gives a polite cheer. Elliot steps into the parlor.)

ELLIOT

How nice. I should come here more often.

RUTH

Are you gaining weight again?

ELLIOT

And then there's Ruth.

RUTH

It was a *compliment*. You were getting too skinny.

ELLIOT

Then we went to Italy. You can't stay skinny in Italy.

BROOKS

Which is why I try to focus on the art.

ELLIOT

The art didn't interest me as much as the pasta.

RUTH

Well, I think you look great. I'm happy to see that you've bounced back.

(A moment.)

KYRA

Speaking of food, you should grab something. Don't be shy.

ELLIOT

Oh you don't have to worry about that.

(Luz reenters and approaches to collect Elliot's jacket. He's surprised to see her.)

Oh. Luz. Hello.

LUZ

Mr. Emerson.

(Kyra senses the tension. Luz goes to hang up his jacket. Elliot finds a spot and puts down his satchel.)

KYRA

So, Luz has been pitching in around here. I probably should've called you about it. But she said you didn't need her anymore, so / I thought—

ELLIOT

No, no, that's true. I'm happy that she found work so quickly.

KYRA

I was worried I might've broken some kind of neighborhood protocol.

ELLIOT

Oh gosh, not at all. Luz is wonderful. I'm glad you snapped her up.

KYRA

Okay. Phew.

(Elliot heads for the food.)

You should try the frittata by the way, it's excellent.

ELLIOT

Thanks for the tip. But I am *very* familiar with Luz's frittata.

BROOKS

Hey, Elliot, you should tell Kyra about the aluminum siding.

RUTH	MELISSA	ISAAC
Oh for godsakes.	Why, Brooks?	Engage launch sequence.

ELLIOT

On *this* house? Do you not know about that, Kyra? *(Comes back to the parlor)* Well, this was ages ago, but the doctor who lived here hired a crew *two months* before we were landmarked.

ISAAC

Not *my* guys. This was way before my time.

ELLIOT

I happened to be walking by and I saw them covering the house in aluminum siding. I couldn't believe it!

PENNY

(Always enjoys this story) He couldn't believe it!

ELLIOT

I rang the bell and Dr. Klein answered and I said, "Marty, what the hell are you doing?"

PENNY

(Still amused by it) "Marty, what the hell are you doing?"

ELLIOT

And he said, "We aren't landmarked *yet*! You don't know what my bills are like! And aluminum keeps the heat in!"

PENNY

(Loves the punchline) "Aluminum keeps the heat in!"

ELLIOT

Can you imagine? *Aluminum siding*. On a *Victorian*!

BROOKS

Grab your pitchforks!

ELLIOT

You make fun, but I had to look at that travesty for forty years!

(This comes out angrier than he intends. Beat.)

KYRA

Well, I'm glad we replaced it.

MELISSA

That's right, it's a new era. All hail the queen!

BROOKS

To the queen!

ALAN

Down with aluminum!

RUTH

Cheers.

ISAAC

To Kyra.

PENNY

Welcome, Kyra!

WILLOW

To fresh starts.

(They raise glasses and drink.)

ELLIOT

On that note, we should probably get started.

(Elliot hands out agendas. People find seats. Luz reenters and fills wine glasses. Penny opens a notebook.)

PENNY

(To Kyra) I'm in charge of taking the minutes.

ALAN

Did you meet Dr. Klein? When you were buying this place?

KYRA

No, we dealt with his daughter mostly.

ALAN

He was a real character. Never paid the neighborhood dues. Or donated to block parties. He didn't want to pitch in for *anything*. I bet he socked it to you on the price of the house, right?

(A look between Ruth and Willow.)

KYRA

We thought it was fair. Elliot handled the sale actually.

PENNY

Elliot handles *most* of the sales in this neighborhood.

BROOKS

Eunice repped our house.

ISAAC

Careful, you're gonna set him off again.

ELLIOT

Yes, I lose some business to Eunice. But I get the nicer houses.

BROOKS

Thanks, Elliot.

ELLIOT

Not *your* house. *Your* house is charming.

BROOKS

(To the others) That's real estate talk for "small."

(Kyra notices that Elliot has pulled out a gavel.)

KYRA

Oh, there's a gavel.

MELISSA

Whatever you do, don't touch it. Elliot is very protective of his gavel.

ELLIOT

It belonged to Tom Robey, the Association's first president. This gavel's been handed down— How many years, Penny?

PENNY

Don't make me do math.

ELLIOT

Well, it's many years. And yes, I guard it with my life. *(Bangs the gavel)* I call to order the April meeting of the Vernon Point Neighborhood Association. Let me start by officially welcoming Kyra and thanking her for stepping in on such short notice. Also, for hosting.

KYRA

Luz did most of the food.

WILLOW	ISAAC	ALAN
Thank you, Luz.	It's all delicious.	I love the frittata.

(Luz waves as she heads to the kitchen.)

ELLIOT

And a big thanks to our vice president for putting Kyra's name forward.

MELISSA

I didn't have to twist her arm too hard.

KYRA

She's right, I'm a joiner.

ELLIOT

On a more sensitive note, I should mention Ken Horace. I know it wasn't easy asking him to step off the board, but I want to thank you all for navigating that. Especially to Ruth for taking over as treasurer.

RUTH

Ken left me with quite the mess.

ELLIOT

Rest assured, Ken has agreed to pay back every dollar he drained from our account. And, I'm happy to report, he's back on the wagon.

MELISSA

Here's to Ken and his sobriety.

MOST EVERYONE	WILLOW
(Raises a glass) To Ken.	*(Raises a glass)* To sobriety.

ELLIOT

Back to Kyra. I hope you don't mind, but we usually ask new members to say a little about themselves and why they chose to live in Vernon Point.

ALAN

It's part of the hazing ritual.

KYRA

(A little chuckle) Oh, okay. Well, I think most of you already know, but I'm Kyra Marshall. My family and I moved from Baltimore about nine months ago. We have twin daughters, Carolyn and Bianca. They're ten. I'm sure you've seen them running around the lawn.

WILLOW

They're very sweet.

KYRA

No, they're not, but thank you. We learned about the neighborhood from Melissa actually. My husband Leon is an IP attorney at her firm.

PENNY

What's an IP attorney?

BROOKS

Intellectual property.

(Penny is still not sure what it means.)

KYRA

As for me, I worked in corporate finance for way too long. Now I'm hoping to redefine myself and maybe try something more low key. So I'm thinking of opening a little bookstore.

ALAN	WILLOW	BROOKS
Oh, wow.	Very cool.	We *need* a bookstore.

RUTH

I just go on Amazon.

ELLIOT

And why Vernon Point?

KYRA

Right. Well, obviously it's a beautiful neighborhood. We like that it's part of the city but still feels kinda suburban, with the porches and the— When Elliot showed us around, there were all these kids riding on bikes.

BROOKS

He pays them to do that.

KYRA

When I was growing up, this was exactly the kind of neighborhood I dreamed of living in, which is so corny, but—

ISAAC

No, it's not.

KYRA

Also, we liked how diverse the community was. And how *safe* it felt. Safety was a big thing. And compared to Baltimore—which we loved by the way, but this is more . . . it's like from another era. I mean, obviously, it's landmarked, but . . . Everything is just . . . really *nice*.

MELISSA

She also likes Thai food, *Scrabble*, and good gossip.

PENNY

Oh, you're gonna fit right in.

KYRA

Does that mean I passed?

ELLIOT

It wasn't a test.

BROOKS

It was absolutely a test.

ELLIOT

Thank you, Kyra, that was wonderful.

(Polite applause from the group.)

RUTH

It's not *all* nice. *(Off their looks)* She should know. Not *everything* is nice.

ELLIOT

Okay, Ruth. Next on the agenda is the Landmarks Committee. Which maybe you'd like to join, Kyra. We could use some fresh blood.

KYRA

Oh, maybe. What does that committee do?

MELISSA

It polices the neighbors.

ELLIOT

No, that's not what we— We're mostly a liaison between the neighborhood and the City Landmarks Commission.

MELISSA

And you make damn sure everyone follows the rules.

ELLIOT

Well yes, obviously that's *part* of it, but I wouldn't call that *policing*. Landmarks is maybe more important to me because I've lived here my whole life and I've seen what can happen if we aren't vigilant.

PENNY

Look at Vernon North. That neighborhood's gone now.

ELLIOT

Exactly. All those houses leveled to put up the projects. It was lucky we got landmarked when we did. It put an invisible wall around us. At least in our little citadel, things would stay as they were. *(Back to Kyra)* So, that's the Landmarks Committee.

KYRA

Got it. Thanks.

ELLIOT

The only item I have is just something to flag for now. Some of you may have noticed that the Crawfords are replacing their front porch.

ISAAC

Not *my* job by the way. They made me a lowball offer I couldn't accept. I love my crew too much to do that to them. So if there's an issue, it's probably because they're cutting corners.

ELLIOT

I'm not sure if there's an issue or not. But I did notice a delivery of farmhouse balusters sitting in the Crawfords' driveway this morning. I'm hoping they're not for the porch.

BROOKS

Why not?

ELLIOT

Because farmhouse balusters aren't true to the period or style of the original railing. They'd look ridiculous on that Queen Anne.

MELISSA

But we don't police our neighbors.

ELLIOT

It's not *policing*. If you live here, you've agreed to certain guidelines.

KYRA

I hate to ask, but what exactly are balusters?

ELLIOT

(Chuckles) I'm sorry, Kyra. We should've started with that.

ISAAC

They're the posts that support a railing. They're like spindles but with footings.

KYRA

Okay, I'm gonna nod and pretend I know what that means.

MELISSA

You're gonna learn *so* much useless information here.

ELLIOT

It's not useless. The balusters are important. They hold everything up. A porch'll fall to pieces without the right support.

RUTH

As riveting as this is, may we move on?

ELLIOT

Yeah, okay. Let's table this until we know what the Crawfords are up to. In the meantime, do you want to give the Security report, Alan?

ALAN

Happy to. For those who don't follow the Facebook Group, a few more neighbors have reported packages being stolen from their porches. So we're encouraging everyone to get cameras if they can.

ISAAC

The security van hasn't seen anything?

ALAN

We only have the van from six P.M. to midnight, and most of the thefts happen during the day, when people aren't home.

WILLOW

Maybe we should shift the hours earlier.

BROOKS

Speaking of, our son's bike was stolen from the yard last week.

WILLOW

Oh, no. Poor Luke.

BROOKS

It was our fault. Chaz left the back gate open. I'm always telling him to lock it, but he can never remember.

ELLIOT

Did you report it to the precinct?

BROOKS

They're not really helpful at the precinct. That time our tire was slashed, I went in / there and—

ELLIOT

Still, it's important that there's a record of these things.

BROOKS

I'll have Chaz go in. Cops are nicer to him. I'll let *you* figure out why.

ALAN

(After a slightly awkward silence) So, do we want to consider changing the hours of the security van or—?

RUTH

I wonder if it's because of all the renovations happening. Whenever there's an influx of workmen, there's an uptick in crime.

PENNY

There *is*?

WILLOW

Where did you get *that* statistic?

ISAAC

I hope you're not accusing *my* guys. Because they have enough eyes on them as it is.

RUTH

I didn't say *your* guys. There are lots of workers in the neighborhood.

ISAAC

I think the van should start patrolling when school gets out, because *that's* who's doing the pilfering.

WILLOW

You don't know that.

ISAAC

When are the packages disappearing? Between two and three. It doesn't take Sherlock Holmes to crack the case.

BROOKS

He was all over the Facebook Group with this.

ISAAC

Every day packs of teenagers come strolling through the neighborhood. We're right between the high school and the projects / so . . .

BROOKS

Let's not make assumptions, Isaac.

ISAAC

When was your kid's bike stolen? During the day, right?

BROOKS

We should've locked the gate.

ALAN

So it sounds like we're shifting the security van hours, yes?

(Kyra listens to all of this, riveted and, at times, bemused.)

WILLOW

Can I just— And I know I've said this before, but I feel like we all need to be more careful with our words. Especially on the Facebook Group.

ISAAC

Did you see how many people clicked *like* on my post?

PENNY

I'm not *on* Facebook.

WILLOW

I feel like, mentioning the projects— You might as well have said, "Black kids are roaming the neighborhood."

RUTH

Black kids *are* roaming the neighborhood.

WILLOW

No, they're walking from home to school and back. Nobody's *roaming*.

ISAAC

And they're not all Black by the way. It happens to be a very diverse group of hooligans. So don't make this into something it's not. *(Explains to Kyra)* Every meeting, Willow shakes her finger at us.

WILLOW

That's not fair. I'm just saying what / should be said.

BROOKS

Willow's right, we all have blind spots. We should call this stuff out.

WILLOW

And it doesn't have to get prickly. We're all guilty of misspeaking. Case in point, Alan's comments about Dr. Klein being weird about money.

ALAN

But . . . Dr. Klein *was* weird about money.

WILLOW

Just because it's true doesn't mean it's not anti-Semitic.

ALAN

Anti-Semitic? No, that's not at *all* what [I meant.]

RUTH

What about Elliot's obsession with the aluminum siding?

ELLIOT

I never mentioned Dr. Klein's money, only his aesthetics.

RUTH

Right—crass, tacky Jew.

ELLIOT

That is not what I meant and you know it! Good lord, I feel like we can't say *anything* without someone assuming the worst.

ALAN

In my homeroom last week, I said that a movie was lame and a student accused me of using ableist language.

PENNY

Using *what*?

WILLOW

Because you *were* using ableist language. If the movie was lousy, you should've said it was lousy. There are so many words. Why use the ones that injure people?

ALAN

To be fair, I don't think I *injured* anyone.

PENNY

(Beat) I'm probably not gonna put any of that in the minutes.

(Luz reenters the dining room to tidy up.)

ELLIOT

Was there anything else on Security?

ALAN

Yes, I still haven't gotten an answer about the security van / hours.

KYRA

I might have something. Sorry, Alan. I didn't mean to cut you off.

ALAN

(Resigned now) It doesn't matter.

KYRA

I wasn't gonna bring it up, but since we're talking about security and safety . . . I have some concerns about the corner.

(Luz listens from the dining room, interested.)

ELLIOT

The corner?

KYRA

Right out here. Palmer and Akron? There've been a lot of accidents out there. And near misses. About once a week, give or take.

ELLIOT

Huh.

KYRA

There aren't any stop signs there, so cars come speeding down Palmer, and the ones crossing from Akron don't have time to react, so they keep hitting each other at the intersection. Which is really dangerous. A lot of kids ride bikes out there, so it makes me nervous.

BROOKS

I second that concern.

KYRA

So I was thinking maybe we could apply for stop signs. Or a traffic light? Whatever might remedy that situation.

ELLIOT

(Beat) Wow. First meeting. I love how you're jumping right into things.

MELISSA

That's why we're here. It's good you brought it up.

ELLIOT

The thing is, Palmer Road is the only esplanade in the neighborhood, which is what makes it so special—the pretty boulevard with the grassy median? The unobstructed view?

KYRA

Right. I guess I'm not sure what that means.

ELLIOT

It means you can stand at one end of Palmer and see all the way to the other end, and it's just a clean line of stately homes and trees and nothing else. It's like standing in an old postcard.

KYRA

Uh-huh.

ELLIOT

So, you can understand that sticking up stop signs or, god forbid, traffic lights—how that might diminish the character of the block. I can't imagine that Landmarks would appreciate that kind of change.

KYRA

But there are already stop signs in the / neighborhood.

ELLIOT

On the *side* streets. Not on the esplanade.

KYRA

I see. Obviously I don't want to detract from how beautiful the street is.

ELLIOT

Obviously. It's why you moved here.

KYRA

Well, it's *one* of the reasons. But I think I also mentioned safety.

PENNY

You did. I wrote it down.

KYRA

And I don't know what the solution would be, but I worry for— Honestly, I just don't want my girls getting hit by a car.

ELLIOT

Well, so long as they don't play in the street, they should be fine.

KYRA

(A little chuckle) Um . . .

BROOKS

I just want to chime in. I know your kids are grown, Elliot, so maybe this isn't as much of an issue for you—

ELLIOT

I have grandchildren though. They come to visit and I want them to be safe, same as you. So don't make me out to be the old stick in the mud.

MELISSA

Maybe we could form a committee to explore the options.

ELLIOT

Okay, I'm not sure we need another / committee.

WILLOW

Safety issues come up on the Facebook Group all the time.

KYRA

I can chair that if people are interested.

RUTH

I'm / interested.

BROOKS

I'd sit on that / committee.

WILLOW

Same here.

MELISSA

Great! Would that be okay, Elliot?

ELLIOT

Well, I'm not gonna stop anyone from forming a committee, / but—

MELISSA

Then I move to make Kyra chair of a new Traffic and Safety Committee.

BROOKS

I second.

MELISSA

All those in favor?

ALL EXCEPT ELLIOT

Aye.

MELISSA

Opposed?

(They all look to Elliot.)

ELLIOT

I'm not *opposed*; I just didn't have / time to—

MELISSA

Congratulations, Kyra, you have a committee.

KYRA

Yay. I already feel drunk with power.

(Polite chuckles. Elliot hides his discomfort. Luz, satisfied, heads into the kitchen.)

RUTH

May we move on to the Financial report?

ALAN

Actually, I'm still waiting for a decision on the security van.

(Lights out.)

SCENE 2

Two Weeks Later
The Traffic and Safety Committee Meeting

The parlor. A sunny day. The dining room pocket doors are closed. Kyra, Brooks, Willow and Ruth are looking over a packet of papers.

BROOKS	KYRA	RUTH	WILLOW
How many crashes have there been?	We should also mention the near misses.	We didn't have any of this before that light was put in.	I think the more statistics we include, the better.

WILLOW

I bet we could get the official number of accidents from the precinct.

RUTH

And I'm happy to write a testimonial. An SUV nearly took out my Otis at the curb last week. I yanked his leash so hard I almost broke his neck.

KYRA

(Kyra's phone pings, she glances at it) Sorry. I told the girls not to come down, so they're texting me instead. They're fighting over *Minecraft*. I'll be right back. *(Heads upstairs)*

BROOKS

That's one thing we don't get with an only child. In our house Chaz and I do the bickering. Luke just sits and reads.

WILLOW

Aw, you should have more.

BROOKS

Tell that to my husband. He says we're one and done.

RUTH

Is that why you're bickering?

WILLOW

Don't take her bait, Brooks.

BROOKS

Actually, Chaz *loves* kids. But I'm a travel writer, so I'm often out of town. Which means the bulk of the parenting duties fall on Chaz, which isn't always fun for him. It's a lot of work.

RUTH

Oh I know. My girls *still* exhaust me and they're practically menopausal. *(To Willow)* What about you? Your baby-window is narrowing by the day.

WILLOW

Aw thanks, Ruth. But no, Enoch and I aren't talking about kids just yet.

BROOKS

I wouldn't rush it.

RUTH

Who's *Enoch*?

WILLOW

My partner. You've met them.

RUTH

No, I met the jewelry maker. *Evelyn*.

WILLOW

Yeah, that's them. But they go by Enoch now. *(Waits as Ruth processes this)* Well, go on. You're obviously dying to say something.

RUTH

No. Just . . . now that I think of it, they didn't *seem* like an Evelyn to me. Enoch feels like a better fit.

(Ruth isn't being snarky. It's uncharacteristic. Willow and Brooks aren't sure how to respond. Kyra comes back down and rejoins them.)

KYRA

Sorry. They're still hopped up on Easter candy.

BROOKS

Back to the speed bumps?

KYRA

Yes. Although . . . and I don't want to be a jerk, but they're not actually bumps, they're humps. *(Off their looks)* Speed *humps*. We keep saying *bumps* but they're really *humps*.

RUTH

Speed humps?

KYRA

Yeah, if you look at the packet it shows how a bump and a hump are two different things. You wouldn't put a speed bump on a residential street.

WILLOW

But I've *seen* them.

KYRA

Those are humps. Despite what the signs might say.

RUTH

I've never even *heard* of a speed hump.

BROOKS

I had a few speed humps back in college but those were different.

(He smiles. Ruth looks even more confused.)

KYRA

(Shows them in the packet) Look, *that's* a bump, and *that's* a hump. See how the hump is shorter and wider? It's like a little hill, so it'll slow you down, / but—

RUTH

That's not a speed bump?

KYRA

No, Ruth, look at the pictures. The speed bump is taller and narrower. They go in parking lots and places where people go slow. You can't put a speed bump on a street like this. You hit that thing at full speed, you're gonna launch the car.

WILLOW

So we want to install speed *humps*.

KYRA

Probably not actually.

BROOKS	RUTH	WILLOW
Oh, no.	For godsakes.	Well why not?

KYRA

A hump would mean a lot of extra signage on the street. And Elliot's head would explode.

(Luz enters with two plates of mamon cakes.)

Oh, quick break. Luz made us a little nosh.

RUTH

Nosh. You're funny.

LUZ

It's mamon. Filipino sponge cake. (*To Willow, re: separate plate)* These ones are vegan.

WILLOW	BROOKS	RUTH
These look delicious.	Yum.	I'm not one for sweets.

(Luz sets them out. Brooks and Willow dig in.)

BROOKS

Oh, I had these in Manila. They remind me of *bolo de fubá*.

LUZ

I don't know what that is.

BROOKS

It's a cake. From Brazil. Different continent, but very similar.

RUTH

Tell me, Luz, how's our Felix doing?

LUZ

Felix is good. He and his wife had a baby.

RUTH

No, *how*? It seems like yesterday he was mowing my lawn.

LUZ

How do you think *I* feel? He made me a *grandmother*.

KYRA

I didn't know you had a son.

LUZ

Yeah, Felix. I've mentioned him a couple times.

RUTH

My Lizzy had such a crush. Is he still doing computer stuff?

LUZ

Yes, but don't ask me to explain it. He makes good money though. *(Searches her phone for a photo)* He keeps telling me I don't have to work anymore. But what would I do with myself? It's all I've ever done. Besides, I'd never take his money. *(Hands phone over to Ruth)*

RUTH

Oh, look at that baby! What a charmer! What's his name?

LUZ

Rocket.

RUTH

(Beat—looks up from the phone) Rocket?

LUZ

Yes. Like a rocket ship. But just Rocket.

RUTH

That's what's on the birth certificate?

LUZ

I wasn't consulted.

WILLOW

I think it's a / cool name.

BROOKS

I really like Rocket / as a name.

KYRA

He's adorable. *(Her phone pings again)* These girls are giving me gray hairs. Do you mind breaking it up, Luz?

LUZ

(Beat) No, I don't mind. *(Takes her phone)*

RUTH

Congrats on the grandbaby. He's precious.

LUZ

Thank you. Enjoy the mamon. *(Heads upstairs)*

RUTH

I'll just try a small piece. *(She takes a mamon)*

WILLOW

I love these little plates. I noticed them at the board meeting.

KYRA

You know what's funny about those? When Leon and I were getting married, my mother made us register for china, which was ridiculous because we didn't grow up like that. My mother cleaned hotels most of her life. All our dishes were like, Corelle.

BROOKS

Crazy Daisy plates.

KYRA

Exactly! So it was weird that she thought we needed *china*. And not just plates, but saucers and soup bowls and . . . *all* of it. It obviously *meant* something to her, so we registered. Then we spent twenty years carrying boxes of china from apartment to apartment and never used it.

WILLOW

No?

KYRA

No, because we didn't host like, formal dinners, or whatever. But we have this dining room now, so we had a bunch of family for Easter, and we set out the china and my mother was just . . . *(makes a glowing noise)* I mean, she was happy when the girls were born, but this maybe meant more to her.

BROOKS

Because you finally had a house that matched the dishes?

KYRA

Well, it's kinda gross when you say it like that, but . . . yeah, actually.

RUTH

Why would they name him Rocket? *(Off their looks)* Have we run out of names? Is that what's happened? We're resorting to naming children after random objects now? They might as well call him Doorknob. Or *Taco*.

KYRA

That's his middle name actually.

RUTH

Ha! Rocket Taco!

(They laugh. Ruth continues to eat her mamon.)

BROOKS

Did you ever find out why Elliot let her go?

KYRA

I didn't ask.

BROOKS

Why not? I thought you *liked* gossip?

RUTH

Who cares what happened? Luz is amazing and Kyra's lucky to have her.

WILLOW

Agreed.

RUTH

I have to say though, I'm surprised you didn't want a *white* maid.

KYRA

(Beat) What'd you / just say?

BROOKS

(Laughs) Oh my / god.

WILLOW

I am so sorry, Kyra.

RUTH

What? Is that wrong to say?

WILLOW

Yes, Ruth, that's wrong to say!

RUTH

Why? It's nothing against Luz. She's a wonderful housekeeper.

KYRA

But you thought I'd prefer a white one.

RUTH

Why not? It would've evened the score a little bit.

KYRA	BROOKS	WILLOW
Evened the score?	Ruth, no.	You have to stop.

RUTH

What's wrong with that? You deserve it.

KYRA

I deserve it. A white maid.

RUTH

I think so.

KYRA

As what, *reparations*?

RUTH

All I'm saying is, it's nice when the wheel of history turns. Why do you think my housekeepers are always German?

BROOKS

Wow.

WILLOW

Is that true?

RUTH

I *insist* on it.

KYRA

As *payback*?

RUTH

Look, I adore my Frieda. She's a good worker, but there are *moments*—if she doesn't get the dog hair off the couch cushions for example—when I need to scold her a little. And I have to confess that when I do . . . it feels good. *Karmically*. I like to imagine my grandmother looking down and saying "Look at that Kraut cleaning her house! Good for you, Rutele!"

BROOKS

My god.

RUTH

You don't have these thoughts?

BROOKS

I don't have a housekeeper.

RUTH

You have that gardener though. Who has a *white* gardener?

KYRA

I'm sure there are lots of white gardeners.

RUTH

In *Norway* maybe.

BROOKS

You're right, our gardener is white. And *Southern* actually. And when he's trimming the hedge, I suppose it *is* satisfying. But not for the reasons you think.

WILLOW

Okay, creeper.

KYRA

Have you *seen* him? He's very attractive.

RUTH

Well good! You *deserve* an attractive white gardener!

BROOKS

You know what? I actually agree with you.

(Ruth takes another mamon. They hear Luz descending the stairs.)

LUZ

Peace restored.

KYRA

Thank you, Luz.

(Luz heads to the kitchen. It's hard to know if she overheard any of their conversation.)

WILLOW

So no to the speed humps. And traffic lights seem like overkill.

KYRA

Stop signs are the only logical choice.

RUTH

Elliot'll be upset no matter *what* we propose.

KYRA

No, I know. I was trying so hard the other night but I couldn't stop myself. I thought, "Oh no, Kyra, this is Baltimore all over again."

BROOKS

Oo, say more.

WILLOW

Yeah, what's *that* story?

KYRA

No, it's not really . . . I was just . . . I was on the board of our co-op and they didn't always . . . appreciate my input, let's say.

RUTH

Some people can't take an opinionated woman.

KYRA

Yeah, that wasn't it though. There were other women there, and they spoke up way more than I did. They just didn't like when *I* spoke up.

RUTH

Ah, I see now.

KYRA

It was a toxic bunch. At one meeting in particular— The building had this big common room that you could reserve for parties and we were debating who got to use the room, and the parameters around *guests*.

BROOKS

It got contentious?

KYRA

Very. And all of this came up because we had thrown the girls a birthday party the week before, so this was obviously about *us* and *our* guests, but no one would say that. And the board president was this awful hag and she was being a total prick about it. Pardon my French.

RUTH

No need, I speak it fluently.

KYRA

So this lady kept digging in, so I pushed back, and in the heat of battle made a few accusations I maybe shouldn't have, and this woman got more and more upset and her face turned red, and then she stopped suddenly. And she looked confused and tried to say something, but it was just this garbled nonsense that came out.

WILLOW

Oh no.

KYRA

Oh yeah, and her whole left side kinda seized up, and her mouth drooped—

RUTH

You gave her a *stroke*?

KYRA

To be fair, she gave *herself* a stroke. But I certainly didn't help matters.

BROOKS

Did she die?

KYRA

She did.

WILLOW

She *died*?

KYRA

Well, not in front of us, but later. At the hospital. I felt terrible.

RUTH

Yeah, because you killed a woman.

KYRA

Needless to say, things got a little awkward with the neighbors after that. So when Leon got the job offer here, I was like, "Yeah, maybe it's time to move and open that bookstore."

BROOKS

That was an excellent story.

KYRA

Thanks.

BROOKS

But why, after all *that*, would you ever say yes to *this*?

KYRA

Because I actually *like* being involved and being a part of the decisions. It's just my personality. The only part I *don't* like . . .

RUTH

Are the strokes?

KYRA

What I don't like is the friction. I'm trying to be better at defusing situations instead of escalating them.

WILLOW

And you think butting heads with Elliot is the way to do that?

BROOKS

Willow has a soft spot. Elliot's essentially her uncle.

WILLOW

He's not my uncle. He was my dad's best friend.

RUTH

I say we just propose the signs. Elliot's only got one vote.

BROOKS

You know that's not true. Penny always votes with him. So do Alan and Isaac. Elliot's got a voting bloc.

KYRA

Do we need the board's permission though? To apply for a stop sign?

WILLOW

The endorsement from the board always helps the case.

KYRA

But we don't technically need it, right? I could hop on the Facebook Group to drum up some support. Maybe pull a list of names together instead. That might be just as persuasive.

RUTH

It'd also make it harder for Elliot to squelch.

WILLOW

What happened to defusing instead of escalating?

KYRA

Isn't checking in with the neighbors just due diligence? And so long as we're not breaking any rules—

BROOKS

I think you should do it.

WILLOW

Because you like stirring the pot.

RUTH

What's the worst that could happen?

(Ruth bites into a third mamon. Lights out.)

SCENE 3

May Meeting
Vernon Point Neighborhood Association

The parlor. The meeting is in progress. Penny takes notes. Melissa is mid-rant.

MELISSA

It doesn't make sense. These people go to the trouble of picking up after their dogs, which—good job, you did the hard part, you put some poop in a bag—but instead of carrying it home, they just—*bloop!*—pop it into my trash barrel. Which may sound fine because it's the *garbage*, but the trash guys don't actually tip the barrels into the truck anymore.

ALAN

That's true, they used to pick up the whole barrel.

MELISSA

Now they just lift out the big bags. So the little turd bombs all fall to the bottom of the barrel. And the guys don't fish those out. So every week *I* have to do it, then transfer the poop to a *big* bag to be collected the *next* week. It's disgusting. I don't have a dog, so why am I handling dog shit?

PENNY

What do you mean, you don't have a dog? I see Bernie walking a corgi every morning. That's not your dog?

MELISSA

No . . . that's not my dog.

(This exchange confuses Penny.)

BROOKS

When I was in Kyoto, people wore these sporty little satchels. For dog poop. They'd just bag it, pop it in, and zip it up.

ELLIOT

Well, I don't think we can ask people to wear *satchels*. I'll put a reminder in the newsletter about pet waste dos and don'ts. Now let's move on.

PENNY

I think I'm next. With some sad news unfortunately. The imam from the mosque—his wife Sidra passed away over the weekend.

WILLOW

Oh, no. She was so lovely.

ELLIOT

She was my chemo buddy. I'd always see her at the infusion center. *(Explains to Kyra)* This was a couple years ago. I'm fine now.

KYRA

Oh. That's . . . [good.] I'm glad to hear that.

RUTH

Ignore him, Kyra. He only mentions cancer when he's looking for sympathy. He knows that the corner's on the agenda, so he's trying to soften us up in advance.

ELLIOT

You're on to me, Ruth. I can never get one by you.

RUTH

That doesn't stop you from trying.

PENNY

Anyway, I thought maybe we could send a floral arrangement to Sidra's family expressing our sympathies.

KYRA	ISAAC	WILLOW
That's a great idea.	That'd be really nice.	For sure we should do that.

RUTH

(A shrug of a noise) Eh.

ELLIOT

(Beat, looks to her) Was there something else, Ruth?

RUTH

I just . . . I have some complicated feelings around the mosque.

MELISSA

Yes, we remember. But could you maybe overlook those feelings so we can send some flowers to the family of a dead lady?

BROOKS

Do they have to come specifically from the board? Can't they just be from whoever wants to be a part of that? Because I'm not sure that I do.

(They all look to Brooks.)

RUTH

Guess I'm not the only one with complicated feelings.

BROOKS

I just get some aggressive vibes from the son. The imam's son. He owns the health food store? He's not the friendliest, let's say. Whenever I walk in there, he gives me a *look*.

ISAAC

What kind of look?

BROOKS

An I-hate-gay-people look.

KYRA

Really? From *Nadeem*? He's always so nice to me.

ALAN

Maybe because you're not gay.

PENNY

The flowers aren't to *Nadeem*; they're to the whole family.

ISAAC

How do you know it's the gay thing? Maybe it's the Black thing.

BROOKS

No. Following me through the store would be the Black thing. Judgy side-eye is the gay thing.

ALAN

Yeah, homophobe makes sense. Since he's Muslim.

WILLOW

Jesus, Alan. What does *that* mean?

ALAN

Doesn't the Quran say homosexuality is an / abomination?

WILLOW

The Quran says a lot of things, so does the Bible, so does the Torah, but most people pick and choose the bits they like / and ignore the rest.

ALAN

No, I know. I was just offering a *theory*.

PENNY

So are we *not* sending flowers?

ELLIOT

I know Nadeem well. We're both members of HAMBA—the Haskell Ave. Merchant and Business Association. He's a really good guy.

KYRA

Yeah, my gut says this is just a misunderstanding.

BROOKS
And I'm sure your gut knows more than my lived experience.

KYRA
Come on, that's not fair.

WILLOW
You should just grab a drink with him.

BROOKS
Well, whatever I say, you bat it away.

ALAN
I don't think Muslims *can* drink.

KYRA
Sorry, I was just taken aback because I consider Nadeem a friend and—

WILLOW
Oh, I didn't realize you were such an expert on Islam.

BROOKS
Well, maybe he's nicer to friends than he is to random homosexuals.

ALAN
I'm not an *expert*. I've just heard that booze is forbidden.

PENNY
Oh for cripes' sake, *I'll* send the flowers! *(Beat)* The card'll say, "Condolences from your caring neighbors." And whoever wants to pitch in can pitch in.

ELLIOT
Thank you, Penny. Perfect solution.

RUTH
I'm not pitching in.

WILLOW
Yes, we know.

ISAAC
No kidding, Ruth.

MELISSA
You made that very clear.

ELLIOT

Let's move on to Security.

KYRA

Is that us or—?

ELLIOT

No, you're next. I gave Traffic and Safety its own line on / the agenda.

KYRA

Oh, I see it now. Sorry, I'm a little eager.

ELLIOT

So I'm realizing.

ALAN

Just a quick report. The new van hours seem to be working out, but we still had a few more stolen Amazon boxes this month.

BROOKS

Also, Luke's skateboard was swiped from our yard. Chaz keeps forgetting to lock that damn gate.

ISAAC

I might have a lead on all this actually. I'm just gonna hand these out. *(Passes printouts around the group)*

ALAN

I wasn't quite finished with / my report.

ISAAC

I saw a couple skells on the esplanade last week. Real shady types. I've seen them before, loitering and checking out the houses.

MELISSA

They were standing on the esplanade?

ISAAC

Sitting, but yeah. It was kinda fishy so I took these photos. I thought I'd post them on the Facebook Group, so folks can be on the lookout.

WILLOW

Oh, that would really not be cool, Isaac. These boys are like, fourteen.

ISAAC

So? If they're old enough to steal packages—

KYRA

But you didn't see them stealing, you saw them sitting on the grass.

ISAAC

Okay, but these kids were *eyeing* the houses.

MELISSA

Were they though? In this photo they're just looking at a *tree*.

ISAAC

In *that* one, yeah, but there are others where / you can see—

WILLOW

This feels really profiley to me.

BROOKS

For those who wondered, *this* is the Black thing.

ISAAC

Hey, I'm just following the see-something-say-something policy.

ELLIOT

If you put these online, the families will find out, and people will go berserk, so let's not fuel that particular fire. Isaac, please don't post these photos.

ISAAC

Okay. Message received. Let the crime spree continue.

ELLIOT

Anything else on Security?

ALAN

No, but I would like the minutes to reflect that I don't, in fact, think that all Muslims hate gay people.

(Willow isn't convinced. Penny makes a note. Luz enters the dining room from the kitchen.)

ELLIOT

Which brings us to Traffic and Safety.

KYRA	RUTH	BROOKS
Here we go.	Finally.	I'll get the easel.

(Ruth hands out materials. Willow and Brooks set up an easel with a street diagram. Luz refills wine glasses over the following.)

ISAAC

I love when someone breaks out an easel.

MELISSA

(Re: the wine) Yay, reinforcements. Thank you, Luz.

KYRA

So these packets lay out the research we did regarding the car accidents at the corner and some possible options to best address the issue. *(Moves to the diagram)* Just as a reminder, to avoid this light up here on Haskell, cars are cutting down these side streets and turning onto Palmer.

RUTH

Which is causing all the trouble.

KYRA

So our committee decided that the least meddlesome solution is to put stop signs . . . *(Indicates corners on diagram)* here, here, and here. We posted in the Facebook Group to get feedback and the response was overwhelmingly in favor of the signs. With all that, we were hoping to get a letter of support from the board to submit with our application.

ELLIOT

That's great. Thank you, Kyra. I know we all really appreciate the work your committee put into this. Should we open it up for discussion?

PENNY

I wondered if you had considered speed bumps at all?

RUTH

They're humps, actually.

PENNY

They're *what*?

RUTH

Speed *bumps*. And yes, we looked into them. As well as traffic lights.

KYRA

But they all come with extra signage, so stop signs seemed like the best compromise. And the Facebook Group was on board with that.

ELLIOT

Yes, about that— You were incredibly gracious to jump onto the board when we needed you, Kyra, but it happened so quickly that we neglected to explain our feelings on the Facebook Group.

KYRA

Ah, okay. I just assumed that it was a way for neighbors to connect.

ELLIOT

It *can* be, yes, but it's also easy to rile that gang up. Which is why we've asked Isaac to tone down his comments on there.

ISAAC

I think people find my perspective refreshing.

MELISSA

I don't think they do.

KYRA

I just thought of it as an easy way to take the temperature of the whole community, instead of just the nine people in this room.

ELLIOT

Right, but if things are being presented in a skewed way then it's easy to sway opinions. And then we have factions and misinformation / and—

KYRA

Did you *read* the discussion? Because that's not at all / what happened.

ELLIOT

I did read the discussion, and I have to say, I felt that certain sides of the issue weren't being fairly represented.

WILLOW

You should've chimed in, Elliot.

ELLIOT

No, board issues aren't meant to be hashed out on Facebook.

KYRA

But this isn't a *board* issue, it's a *community* issue.

ELLIOT

Everything we *do* on the board is a community issue, that's *why* we're here. And it's best to do the messy work in this smaller group, so we can present things as a united front. But you obviously had other plans.

KYRA

What do you mean?

ELLIOT

Honestly? It felt like you were rallying the troops a bit.

KYRA

No, that's not at all / what I was [doing.]

ELLIOT

Which puts any opposing views at an extreme disadvantage. So now if things *don't* go your way, these people are going to be upset. Which is what happens when you kick a hornet's nest.

KYRA

Hornet's nest? What are you even *talking* ab—? *(Beat, "keep it together")* Sorry. All due respect, it's not a hornet's nest. Everyone *wants* the signs.

ELLIOT

But they don't. That's the problem. You keep making assumptions.

KYRA

I have the names of over two hundred neighbors who agree / that—

ELLIOT

And I have the names of three hundred and fifteen who *don't*. *(Beat—he passes out papers of his own)* Not everyone's on social media. There are a lot of Vernon Point residents, older ones especially, who don't engage in online chitchat, but do happen to have a deep commitment to historical preservation.

RUTH

What *is* this?

ELLIOT

I felt that a portion of the community wasn't being heard from in regard to this issue, so I knocked on doors and rallied a few troops of my own.

WILLOW

Is this a *petition*?

ELLIOT

You are of course welcome to apply for stop signs and submit the names of all your Facebook friends who endorse your application. You're allowed to do that, Kyra. Just as I'm allowed to submit a *protest* to that application with my *opposing* signatures, as well as letters of support from our assemblyman, two state reps, and the executive director of the city's historical society, with whom, every Friday, I play pickleball.

BROOKS

Damn.

ISAAC

Luz, could I get another splash?

(He does.)

ELLIOT

I know that you're new to the board, Kyra, but we try not to steamroll each other in here.

KYRA

And this packet of yours isn't steamrolling?

ELLIOT

No, it's counterpunching. And it could've been avoided if you had just kept the conversation among us instead of going behind / my back.

KYRA

I was just trying to include the rest of the neighborhood.

ELLIOT

No, you were trying to include *part* of the neighborhood. The part that happens to agree with you.

KYRA

Why do I feel like I'm being scolded right now?

ELLIOT

I'm sorry, that's not my intention. But as the president, it's my job to crack the— I need to / keep things in order.

KYRA

The *whip*? Crack the *whip*?

BROOKS

Oh you don't wanna say *that*.

ELLIOT

Crack down on *protocol*, is what I was going to say.

KYRA

Oh, okay. *Protocol*.

ELLIOT

You may not realize *why* we do things the way we do here, Kyra. But the truth is, we do it this way because that's what *works*. It's what's *always* worked. Going all the way back to Tom Robey and the first Association.

KYRA

Can we vote?

ELLIOT

I have a responsibility to keep things / running smoothly.

KYRA

(So calm now) I understand, Elliot. I really do. We don't need to argue about this. Let's just vote and see where we land.

PENNY

I'm not sure what we're voting on.

KYRA

I'd still like a letter of support from the board. Obviously Elliot doesn't think the stop signs are a good idea, but maybe others do.

ELLIOT

Not just me, I have letters from / the—

MELISSA

She wants a vote, Elliot.

ELLIOT

Yes, I heard her. I don't need your help running the meeting. I've been doing this many years.

MELISSA

Yeah, because we don't have term limits.

ELLIOT

Alright, let's not get sidetracked on *that* topic again. Fine, Kyra has made a motion on a letter of support for the proposed stop signs on the corners of Akron and Palmer. All those in favor?

(Kyra raises her hand. A moment. No one else does. This confuses her.)

Opposed?

(Everyone else—many reluctantly—puts a hand up. Kyra smiles in disbelief.)

KYRA

(To other committee members) Wow. You all are *on* the committee.

RUTH

It just seems fruitless / at this point.

BROOKS

He's got the assemblyman and the / historical society—

MELISSA

We usually only get one shot with this kind of thing, Kyra. It's better if we apply with an airtight argument.

(Luz starts to clear plates.)

ELLIOT

This isn't personal. We just have a particular process here. Maybe things were done differently on your board in Baltimore.

KYRA

No, this feels very similar actually.

WILLOW

Maybe there's a solution we haven't thought of yet.

(Luz moves to clear Alan's plate.)

ALAN

Oh, I'm not quite finished with that.

(As he pulls the little plate back, he loses his grip and it falls to the floor and breaks. Kyra's eyes flare. Luz and Alan move to clean it up.)

Dang it. I'm such a klutz.

BROOKS

Is that your wedding china?

KYRA

(Trying to hide her annoyance) It's fine. Accidents happen.

ALAN

I'm so sorry. I can replace it.

KYRA

No, that pattern isn't really available / anymore.

ALAN

(Cleaning up the mess) Oh god, I feel terrible.

KYRA

(To the others) Can I just—? I feel like I should be clear here. I'm still submitting the request. For the stop signs. *(Beat)* If you want to send in your little opposition packet, you go right ahead, but that intersection is dangerous. Someone is gonna get killed out there, but Elliot's more concerned about it looking like a postcard.

ELLIOT

That's not fair. Obviously I don't want anyone getting / hurt.

KYRA

No, I get it, you've made your point. You think a stop sign is uglier than a dead child. I don't. I'm submitting the request. And if you all want a fight, then I say *bring* it.

(Lights out.)

SCENE 4

The Next Day

Parlor. Luz is at the secretary desk looking for something. Kyra enters from the kitchen with a stuffed and sealed manila envelope. She also has a duffel bag of kids' soccer equipment.

LUZ

I found the stamps. *(Hands them to Kyra)* I can run that up to the mailbox if you want.

KYRA

(Puts down duffel bag) I'll just do it on the way to soccer. It'll be cathartic.

(Kyra is putting stamps on the package when the doorbell rings. Luz goes to answer the door. It's Isaac and Penny.)

PENNY

Hello, Luz.

ISAAC

Is Kyra home by any chance?

LUZ

Oh. Um, she's about to bring the girls to soccer, actually.

KYRA

It's okay, you can let them in.

(She closes up the desk as Isaac and Penny are let in. Kyra isn't overly warm to them.)

ISAAC

Hey. Sorry to pop by unannounced. We'll be really quick.

KYRA

(To Luz) Can you just tell the girls to sit tight? I'll be right there.

(Luz heads to the kitchen.)

How are you doing, Penny?

PENNY

Not great actually. I've got another migraine. Any shift in the weather.

KYRA

(Regards them) So what's up?

ISAAC

We just wanted to touch base about last night. Since the meeting was . . .

KYRA

Kinda fucked up?

ISAAC

(Chuckles) Not the phrase I was gonna use but . . . yeah.

PENNY

We mostly wanted you to know that we *like* the stop sign idea.

KYRA

Huh. Well, that's confusing. Since you voted *against* it.

ISAAC

No, we know. But we *had* to. We want the signs out there though. We just wonder if you could maybe press pause on sending the application.

KYRA

Why would I do that? What *is* this? Did Elliot ask you to / come here?

PENNY

Oh god no. If he knew we were here, he'd be furious.

ISAAC

(Notices the package) Is that it there?

KYRA

Sorry, can you get to whatever this is? My girls are waiting in the car.

ISAAC

It's a little touchy, but . . . you know how Ruth was joking about Elliot's cancer, and how he said it was years ago, but he was fine? Well, all that was true. It *was* years ago and he *was* fine. But he's not now. Which Ruth doesn't know. He's not really telling anyone.

PENNY

I only know because I answer Elliot's phones at the office, and sometimes I overhear things. I'm not trying to, it just happens.

ISAAC

He was in remission for a stretch, but it's back. My wife is his oncologist, and she's not really allowed to say anything, but I could tell something was going on. So I went to Elliot and dragged it out of him.

KYRA

(Confused) You're married to an oncologist?

ISAAC

(Beat) Damn, why'd you ask it like that? I can't be married to a doctor?

KYRA

(Backpedals) No, of course you can. I didn't mean it the way it / came out.

ISAAC

I just told you Elliot was sick, and your big takeaway is my *wife*?

KYRA

(Her phone pings, she looks at it) Sorry, the girls are getting impatient.

PENNY

Anyway, Elliot's back in treatment, but . . . the situation isn't great. Same thing happened with my husband. He was good for a while, but then he took that last turn—

ISAAC

Which is why we were hoping you might hold off on the application. We like the stop signs. But maybe we can revisit them a little later.

KYRA

When he's dead, you mean?

PENNY

(Beat) Golly, you get right to the point.

(Kyra's phone pings again. She texts back while talking at the same time.)

KYRA

Sorry, last night was kinda rough, and this is a lot of new information. *(Looks up from her phone)* But he's not *pretending*, right? To be sick? So I'll drop the request?

ISAAC

Pretending? What the hell, / Kyra?

KYRA

I know, that was a gross thing to ask.

ISAAC

I just told you that my wife is treating him.

KYRA

No, I know, sorry. It's just hard to let go of how tricky he is. And Brooks had mentioned that you two are part of Elliot's voting bloc, / so—

PENNY

What voting bloc?

ISAAC

No, he's not pretending. And we didn't come here to *lie* for him.

KYRA

Of course not. I'm sorry. Obviously it's awful what he's going through.

PENNY

Exactly. So hopefully this can be kept between us. We just wanted you to know what was really going on last night. With *us*, at least.

(Car horn from the driveway.)

KYRA

That's the girls, so I should . . .

ISAAC

Yeah, we'll get out of your hair. We just wanted you to have all the pertinent info so you could make an informed decision.

PENNY

Good luck at the soccer game. I hope they win.

KYRA

Oh, they never do. But thank you.

(Isaac and Penny go. A moment. Luz reenters.)

Did you hear any of that? *(Luz nods)* Did you know Elliot was sick?

LUZ

No. Maybe it's new.

KYRA

Or maybe it's not real.

LUZ

(Beat) You're still gonna mail that package though, right? *(No response)* Mr. Emerson would mail it. If the roles were reversed.

KYRA

(Smiles) I hadn't pegged you as a troublemaker, Luz. Is that why you were fired?

LUZ

No. I was never a troublemaker. It's kinda new for me. *(Beat)* And I wasn't fired.

KYRA

Okay.

LUZ

Don't back down. Please. Mr. Emerson should know how it feels to not get his way. I'd like for him to experience that once before he dies.

(A moment. Out in the driveway, the girls honk the horn. Then they lean on it—a prolonged blare. Lights out.)

SCENE 5

June Meeting
Vernon Point Neighborhood Association

Parlor. Everyone but Penny is here. It's storming. Lightning and thunder outside.

ELLIOT

So I've officially confirmed that the Crawfords did *not*, in fact, go through the city to get their porch approved. And the new balusters are not only historically inappropriate, they're from Home Depot.

BROOKS	ALAN	MELISSA
Scandalous.	Uh-oh.	Not Home Depot.
RUTH	ISAAC	WILLOW
What's Home Depot?	That's not good.	Oh no.

ELLIOT

Unfortunately, we're now obligated to report the violation. Which means they'll have to redo the porch or face fines from Landmarks.

KYRA

Doesn't that feel cruel though? I assume that the whole point of their redoing the porch was to add that ramp. For the wheelchair.

ELLIOT

This isn't about the *ramp*. Obviously Mrs. Crawford needs access to her home. This is about the *balusters*.

RUTH

Sure it is.

(The doorbell rings. Luz crosses to answer it.)

ALAN

I'm more surprised that they put the ramp right in *front* of the house instead of on the side by the driveway.

WILLOW

Because you don't want to see a lady in a wheelchair?

ALAN

No, because it'd be a shorter distance for her to travel.

(Flash of lightning. Luz lets Penny in. Penny has an umbrella and is wet from the rain.)

ALAN

Why would you say I don't want to see a lady in a wheelchair?

PENNY

It's a mess out there. I don't want to drip on your floor.

ELLIOT

This wasn't meant to be a big discussion. Let's just move on.

LUZ

It's fine, I have towels for that. Come on in.

(Thunder. Luz hangs up Penny's jacket. Ruth is sitting in Penny's usual seat. Penny, annoyed by this, has to sit somewhere else.)

PENNY

Sorry, I'm late. This storm has my head banging like a tom-tom, and I'm still waiting for my pills to kick in. *(Settles in and takes out her notebook)*

ELLIOT

I think we're up to Security. Alan?

ALAN

Right, okay. Well, I don't have a lot this month / but—

RUTH

Could I jump in here? Because I have a *very* interesting update.

ALAN

(Disbelief) Every. Time. The minute I start talking someone cuts / me off.

RUTH

I'm sorry, Alan. I just have an update on the porch pirates.

BROOKS

I thought we had decided to drop that.

RUTH

But this is a *development*. I saw the boys on the grass a couple days ago when I was walking the dog, and I heard them whispering.

ISAAC

Conspiring, right? Just like I said!

RUTH

But it *wasn't*. They weren't *planning a crime*, they were debating about the houses. The taller boy was pointing at the Morrisseys' and saying, "That one's *mine*, that's *my* house, I'm gonna live *there* one day."

WILLOW

No way.

RUTH

And the other one talked about how he and his sisters would each have their own room, and they'd all have en suite bathrooms.

BROOKS

Is that what he said? *En suite*?

RUTH

French. Can you imagine?

KYRA

So they weren't stealing packages, they were just admiring the houses.

MELISSA

Actually, I think they were doing *both*. *(Off their looks)* Sorry. Maybe those boys *are* in fact French-speaking architecture buffs, but they're also *thieves*. I know because we finally installed security cameras. I have footage of them swiping a box off my porch.

KYRA

Well that's disappointing.

ISAAC

Vindication.

RUTH

No need to gloat.

WILLOW

What was in the box?

MELISSA

A Squatty Potty. Bailey ordered it.

BROOKS

I first used a Squatty Potty in Marrakech. Instant convert.

(Penny is confused by all of this. Lightning.)

PENNY

Who's Bailey?

MELISSA

Bailey is my wife.

(Thunder.)

ELLIOT

Did you forward the footage to the precinct?

MELISSA

I'm not sure I want to involve the police. They're just kids acting stupid.

ISAAC

I could talk to them instead. The boys. I can catch them on the way to school and say, "Hey numb nuts, we got you on camera. Cut the shit."

WILLOW

I like that idea better.

ISAAC

I did the same nonsense as a kid. My father found out, beat my ass, and that was the end of it.

KYRA

Well I hope you're not gonna beat their asses.

RUTH

I hope they don't beat his.

ISAAC

No one's beating anyone's ass.

BROOKS

Unless the cops get involved. Then all bets are off.

MELISSA

I'm gonna hold on to the videos for now. Isaac can talk to them.

ELLIOT

Well, it's not what I'd do, but let's move on.

PENNY

(Looks to Melissa) Since when do you have a wife?

MELISSA

Since ten years ago.

ELLIOT

Okay. Alan, are you ready to—?

ALAN

Yes, it's a really quick report, I / promise.

MELISSA

Actually, I wasn't quite finished. Sorry, Alan. I also wanted to follow up on the dog poop situation.

(Defeated, Alan heads to the dining room to refill his plate.)

ELLIOT

Did you see the newsletter? I laid out all the rules.

MELISSA

Yes, it was very clear. Which made it all the more baffling when I found a little shit bag at the bottom of my barrel this morning.

ISAAC

(Chuckles) Oh no.

MELISSA

Luckily I remembered my cameras. One of them is aimed down my driveway, with a clear shot of the trash barrels. And the culprit.

(She passes her phone. Some folks gather around to look at the clip.)

BROOKS

Oh, there they are!

KYRA

The quality of the image is so good / on this.

WILLOW

Wait, is that . . . ? Oh no, is this Otis?

(Flash of lightning.)

ISAAC

Who's Otis?

BROOKS

Otis is Ruth's dog.

(Thunder. Everyone looks to Ruth.)

KYRA

Is this you, Ruth?

WILLOW

Of course it is, look at the rabbit fur jacket!

RUTH

I was running late and *had* to dump the poop. I'm sorry. It was *one* time.

MELISSA

But it wasn't one time. We've had the cameras a week now. And every morning you come up my driveway and drop your shit in my can.

BROOKS

Brazen.

RUTH

You know what? Fine, *guilty*. When Otis does his business, it's usually on Melissa's curb strip. And yes, I want to get rid of it quickly.

ELLIOT

(Disappointed) Oh, Ruth.

RUTH

I see a lot of people on my walks. I'm a neighborhood representative. I can't have a bag of shit in my hand!

ELLIOT

For godsakes, just carry your poop home like a civilized human.

RUTH

Fine. But I don't appreciate being ambushed like this.

MELISSA

Then you're really not gonna like the gift I left on your porch.

ALAN

(Chuckles as he returns with snacks) That's fantastic.

ELLIOT

Alright, Ruth has been properly chastised. Can we please move on?

PENNY

Actually, I have something to say on this topic.

ELLIOT

Really? On *this* topic?

PENNY

I'd just like to remind us that everyone in this room is a decent person. We wouldn't be here if we didn't care about our neighbors. At the same time, no one is perfect, and sometimes people make mistakes.

MELISSA

Is this about you thinking that I was the other Melissa?

BROOKS

What other Melissa?

KYRA

Melissa Kahn.

RUTH

The Indian lady?

KYRA

She's Pakistani actually.

MELISSA

Honestly, Penny? It's not a big deal.

PENNY

Well, to me it is. And I really wish you had told me sooner instead of chalking it up to "Daffy old lady can't tell her Asians apart."

MELISSA

Well . . . [that *is* kinda what happened.]

PENNY

No, I never thought you *looked* alike. It was just, I met Bernie at an event and he kept talking about his wife Melissa and you were the only Melissa in the neighborhood I knew, so I just assumed that you were his wife.

ELLIOT

I think we should probably / push on.

PENNY

Then I met the *other* Melissa a long time after that and someone had just mentioned that there was a *lesbian* Melissa in the neighborhood—

WILLOW

Alan probably.

ALAN

What the hell, Willow?

PENNY

So everything just got swapped around in my head. And I'm sorry about that. But it was an honest mistake.

MELISSA

Okay.

PENNY

Whenever I ask after Bernie, you say he's fine. And the other Melissa says the same thing when I ask after her wife. Neither of you correct me.

MELISSA

Well, it's not really our job to teach you how / not to [mix us up.]

PENNY

Who said anything about a job? It's common courtesy.

ELLIOT

We have a very full agenda, folks.

PENNY

Yes, and I want to get through it more than anyone, but I just have to say that more and more I've been feeling made fun of in this room.

KYRA

No one is making fun of you.

PENNY

No, they *are*, and not *just* me. Any of us over a certain age.

MELISSA

I'm not sure what you want here, Penny.

PENNY

Well, an apology would be nice.

MELISSA

Wow. That makes *two* old white ladies dumping their shit on me today.

PENNY

I'm not dumping *anything* on you.

MELISSA

Penny, stop. I'm not apologizing. Now let's move on.

PENNY

(She can't believe it) But I'm telling you that you hurt my feelings.

MELISSA

Then we're even.

PENNY

Except *I* apologized.

MELISSA

As you should've. I don't owe you that.

(Lightning flash.)

PENNY

Oh, okay. In that case, Melissa, you can just go . . . *(Not used to swearing)* . . . go shit-fuck the goddamn hell off yourself.

(Thunder. The others are as confused as they are surprised by Penny's outburst.)

RUTH

Well said.

PENNY

I'm sorry. I didn't mean to [cuss.] Let's just finish the meeting.

ELLIOT

Great idea. Alan, would you like to wrap up Security?

ALAN

No thank you. *(Continues eating)*

ELLIOT

Perfect. Brooks, you wanted to talk about meeting protocol?

BROOKS

Yes, I just wanna remind everyone that whatever we *say* in here is supposed to *stay* in here. Because that's apparently not happening. I went into the health food store this week, and Nadeem glared at me—

WILLOW

Why do you keep going in there?

BROOKS

Because I needed flaxseed. Where else am I supposed to get *flaxseed*?

RUTH

Maybe that pretty gardener of yours could plant it.

BROOKS

The point is, Nadeem *glared* at me, then walked over and said, "I heard you refused to pitch in for my mother's funeral flowers."

ISAAC

How would he even know that?

BROOKS

Exactly *my* question. I know that he has friends in this room . . .

ELLIOT	KYRA
I certainly didn't mention it.	I didn't say a word to him.

BROOKS

Well, *someone* did. Which made for a very awkward encounter.

ALAN

Oo, it's like a game of *Clue*.

BROOKS

I'm not asking for a confession, I just want everyone to know that it happened, and it shouldn't have.

(Penny tries to take the minutes, but the more the storm rages, the worse her migraine gets.)

KYRA

Did you maybe mention the flowers to your husband?

(Brooks looks confused. Lightning.)

I only ask because I've seen Chaz in the health food store a few times, and he and Nadeem are always yukking it up at the counter. I know you think that Nadeem hates gay people—

WILLOW

That's also what Alan thinks.

ALAN

No it isn't. Why do you keep saying that?

KYRA

Chaz and Nadeem seem to get along like gangbusters.

(This is news to Brooks. Thunder.)

BROOKS

Chaz wouldn't have said anything.

KYRA

So you *did* mention the flowers. Even though what we *say* in here is supposed to *stay* in here.

BROOKS

Obviously we talk to our spouses about the board.

MELISSA

I don't. I've *tried*, but Bailey finds it triggering.

ELLIOT

Okay, mystery solved. Was there anything else, Brooks?

BROOKS

(Beat) No, that was it.

ALAN

I have something else actually. I'd like to ask Willow if she has a problem with me.

ELLIOT

Alan, please . . .

ALAN

No, she's always got a comment and I'm tired of it.

RUTH

To be fair, she's got a comment for everyone.

ALAN

Maybe, but I get the brunt of them. And she doesn't pull her punches the way she does with everyone else. I'm obviously the safest target.

WILLOW

Because you're a white guy, you mean?

ALAN

The only reason you let Elliot off the hook is that he's old.

ELLIOT

Rude.

ALAN

Every meeting you imply that I'm homophobic or racist / or—

WILLOW

We all hold each other accountable. No one is singling anyone / out.

ALAN

I work hard to show everyone respect. Do I always say the right thing? No, sometimes I bungle it. But I'm never not *trying* to do better.

KYRA

Which is what matters.

ALAN

I'm not sure it is. Because no matter *what* I say, people seem annoyed by me. Which is hard, because I used to be a well-liked person. It's like, one day everyone got together and decided, "You know what? We don't like Alan anymore." And I have no idea what I did. But I can feel it. I can't open my mouth without someone calling me out for some random infraction. My students especially. Do you know how humiliating that is? To be reprimanded by children?

ISAAC

That's what you get for working at a private school.

ALAN

For all their talk of tolerance, this is an incredibly *in*-tolerant generation.

WILLOW

Aren't you gonna gavel this, Elliot?

ELLIOT

(Enjoying this) No, I don't think I am.

ALAN

(Getting worked up) They're all about acceptance and everyone's fluid—which is great, obviously—and yet their *opinions* are set in stone, black and white. No nuance. No grace for anyone who doesn't behave exactly like they want them to behave. Step out of line and you're done. Which, okay, I get if you're a big racist or a sexual predator or whatever, but the occasional slip of the tongue doesn't— [make me a bad person.] We're not all *monsters*! We're not all Harvey Fierstein, okay?!

RUTH

Oh no, what'd *he* do?

(Lightning flash.)

WILLOW

Weinstein. We're not all Harvey *Weinstein*. You said *Fierstein*.

(Thunder.)

ALAN

I said Fierstein?

WILLOW

It doesn't matter.

ALAN

But it *does*! I can tell from your face! To you, mixing up Weinstein and Fierstein is probably some kind of anti-Semitic microaggression.

WILLOW

I mean . . . [it kinda is.]

ALAN

I'm not a bigot, Willow! My wife is Jewish! My son was adopted from *Ethiopia*! And my daughter from *Colombia*! My brother is *gay* and his partner is *Bhutanese*. You should come to my house at Thanksgiving, it's like the goddamn League of Nations over there!

WILLOW

What a hero. You want a medal?

ALAN

No, I don't want a medal. I just want to stop feeling guilty. Because I do what I'm *supposed* to. I learn the right phrases, and try to be an *ally*, and memorize *pronouns*, but it's never enough. The new stuff keeps coming.

MELISSA

May *I* gavel?

ELLIOT

No, you may not.

ALAN

And people aren't patient. They just want you to—*snap*!—be another person. If not, you're off the list. So I try to keep up, but it's *exhausting*.

KYRA

Well, yeah, important work can be / exhausting.

ALAN

But what's the point if it never ends? I feel like Sisyphus. And maybe I'm tired of pushing the rock. I'm a good person! Better than *most*. Why can't that be enough? I'm *middle-aged*. Maybe I'm fully cooked. Maybe I just want to be who I am and not feel *shitty* about it.

WILLOW

I understand, Alan. And I'm sorry the social reckoning has been so hard on you.

ALAN

Well, now you're just being sarcastic.

WILLOW

Because I don't think you realize how much privilege you just spewed. Look around the room. Then maybe apologize.

ISAAC

Can we stop with this?

PENNY	RUTH	ELLIOT
I would like that.	Yes, please.	Thank you.

KYRA	MELISSA	BROOKS
Glad *you* said it.	I second.	*Yes*, let's.

ISAAC

People still like you, Alan. *I* do at least. I *will* say, I like you a little less after the dumb shit you just said, but I still like you. Bit of advice though. That sad little rant? You gotta keep that nonsense to yourself, dude. Because nobody cares. Not about you. I'm sorry, but that's where we are. You wanna complain? Call up your butthurt lefty white guy buddies and commiserate with *them*. Because no one else gives a shit.

ALAN

Now you sound like my wife.

(Flash of lightning.)

ISAAC

And Willow, I like you too. Not as much as I like Alan, but I *do* like you. That said, I don't dig you calling out other people on their privilege when you're a white lady with a five-bedroom Victorian. Some of us weren't lucky enough to inherit a house. Or a trust fund.

WILLOW

Who said I had a trust fund?

(She looks to Elliot. Thunder.)

ISAAC

My point is, you've been handed more than most people. Including your seat on this board. Your dad passed and Uncle Elliot gave you his spot.

WILLOW

He's not my uncle.

ELLIOT

Okay, now I'll gavel.

(He does. Penny winces at the sound. Luz comes in to clear empty plates.)

WILLOW

I *acknowledge* my privilege, and I welcome having it checked. At the same time, I try to use my privilege to lift up others.

RUTH

By working at PETA? I'm sure that cats everywhere appreciate all you've done for them.

WILLOW

PETA isn't just *cats*!

ISAAC

I think it's awesome that you protect animals. They don't have a voice after all. But the rest of us? We do. And we're not a shy bunch. If anyone wants an apology from Alan, they can ask for it themselves. We don't need you to be our savior in here.

WILLOW

(Tearing up now) Oh my god, of *course* not. Is that what you think? Because that is like, the *last* thing I'd ever want to— That is not at *all* how I see myself.

ISAAC

Are you . . . Are you *crying*?

WILLOW

(She is) I'm sorry. I didn't mean to— [make this about myself.]

KYRA	BROOKS	MELISSA
Oh, Willow.	Here we go.	Girl, no. Don't do that.

BROOKS

What'd I say? It was only a matter of time, right?

MELISSA

Who had the June meeting?

ISAAC

I did. Pay up, suckers.

KYRA

I don't have cash. You good with Venmo?

ISAAC

Yeah, either Venmo or Zelle.

(Melissa and Brooks each pass twenty bucks to Isaac. Kyra sends him money from her phone.)

ELLIOT

What is happening right now?

BROOKS

We had a WGT pool.

RUTH

WGT?

KYRA

White Girl Tears. Sorry, Willow.

(Luz quietly slips Isaac twenty bucks. Yes, she was also in on the pool.)

WILLOW

No, I get it. I shouldn't have centered myself like that. Sorry, you guys.

ALAN

You know, not everyone here is a "guy." Maybe in the future you could use a more gender-neutral term, like *folks* or *friends*.

ELLIOT

Okay, in the spirit of getting this train back on the tracks, I want to reiterate what Penny said about everyone here being a decent person.

RUTH

The more it's said, the less I'm convinced.

PENNY

I'm gonna go. This migraine's getting worse. And you people are nuts.

MELISSA

Luz, can you get her jacket?

(Lightning. Penny heads for the foyer. Luz goes to get her jacket and umbrella. Thunder.)

ELLIOT

Alright, I think we're up to Traffic and Safety.

KYRA

Thanks, Elliot. Not a lot to report. As you know from my email last month, I decided to not file the stop sign request.

ELLIOT

Which, as I said, I very much appreciated. I know that we all have strong opinions in here—but I'm always grateful when cooler heads prevail.

(In the foyer, Luz helps Penny into her jacket.)

KYRA

Also, it's given me time to consider other ways to address the issue. Because obviously it's still a really dangerous intersection.

ELLIOT

Well, I don't think we need to relitigate / all that.

KYRA

And what I realized was, we were spending all this energy trying to solve the issue instead of just removing the *cause* of it.

ALAN

'Night, Penny.

(Lightning. Penny goes. Luz turns her attention back to the discussion. Thunder.)

ELLIOT

What do you mean the *cause* of it?

KYRA

If drivers are coming down Palmer to avoid the new light on Haskell, then why not just ask to have that light *removed*? Say, "Hey city, you did this thing and it caused some problems, can we just go back to how it was?" That way the corner's safe *and* we keep our unobstructed view.

RUTH

Well there ya go, the perfect solution.

ELLIOT

Well, yes, except . . .

KYRA

Except what?

ELLIOT

I can't imagine that the city would agree to that. They obviously put that light on Haskell for a *reason*. They didn't / just—

MELISSA

You're getting your way, Elliot. Take the win.

ELLIOT

But why open a whole new can of worms?

KYRA

Okay, now I'm just confused. I've come up with a perfectly valid plan B. Why are you *still* pushing back?!

ELLIOT

Because the corner isn't a problem!

(From outside, we suddenly hear the blare of a car horn and the screech of tires, followed by the sound of something being hit.)

WILLOW	BROOKS	RUTH
Jesus.	Holy shit.	What *was* that?

(Lightning and thunder. Pandemonium as most of them rush to the windows to investigate.)

RUTH

What'd they hit?

ISAAC

(Realizing) Oh fuck.

ALAN

(Also realizing) No no / no no . . .

KYRA

Someone call an ambulance!

(Luz dials her cell phone. Isaac and Alan are the first to run out of the house and into the rain, Kyra and Elliot close behind.)

RUTH

What is it? What happened?

WILLOW

They hit Penny.

(Lightning and thunder. Lights out.)

SCENE 6

A Week Later

Luz shows Elliot into the front parlor. He's carrying an old shoebox. A moment later, Kyra comes in with an enormous floral arrangement.

ELLIOT

Oh my gosh. Would you look at those.

KYRA

Too much?

ELLIOT

Not at all. They're beautiful.

KYRA

(Puts the arrangement down somewhere) I went to the florist we used when the imam's wife passed away. I said that they were

for Penny, and they of course remembered her, so I think they went a little overboard. They offered to deliver it, but—

ELLIOT

No, I wanted to bring it over myself. Penny's daughter flew down from Rochester, so I'd like to check in on her.

KYRA

That'd be nice.

(This is probably when Elliot should make his exit. But he doesn't.)

LUZ

Do you need help getting the flowers to your car?

ELLIOT

Actually, could I trouble you for a cup of tea?

KYRA

Oh, did you want to [stay?]

ELLIOT

Do you mind? I thought we should maybe chat about a couple things.

KYRA

Huh. Okay.

(Kyra and Luz share a look. Elliot heads to the couch. He places the shoebox beside him. Luz heads off to the kitchen.)

Is this why I was assigned the flowers? So you could corner me?

ELLIOT

Well geez, I hope you don't feel *cornered.*

KYRA

What'd you wanna talk about, Elliot?

ELLIOT

Us. The fact that we keep bumping heads. I don't like it. That last meeting was especially rough.

KYRA

Because of Penny, you mean.

ELLIOT

Obviously what happened to Penny was awful.

KYRA

Especially since it didn't have to happen.

ELLIOT

(Beat) Look, I know we've had our disagreements. Which isn't a bad thing. After all, you can't make a pearl without some grit and a little friction.

KYRA

Right.

ELLIOT

But I was hoping we could maybe try to get on the same page. It shouldn't be that hard. Seeing as we're cut from the same cloth.

KYRA

We're what now?

ELLIOT

You don't think so? I just meant, we're both stubborn, we both have strong convictions, and we're both . . . a little cunning.

KYRA

Cunning? No. I'm not cunning. I don't like that word. It implies deceit.

ELLIOT

Well, maybe cunning isn't the right word then.

KYRA

I feel like I'm a fairly straightforward person actually.

ELLIOT

I guess I was thinking about how you went behind my back with the Facebook Group. Plus that thing with Brooks the other night.

KYRA

What thing with Brooks?

ELLIOT

When he accused folks of telling Nadeem about the flowers, and you said that it was probably his husband. I didn't think anyone else knew.

KYRA

That Chaz hangs out at the health food store?

ELLIOT

No, that he and Nadeem are having an affair.

KYRA

(A confused beat) What?

ELLIOT

Oh. You didn't [know?] I assumed you knew.

KYRA

Chaz and Nadeem are having an *affair*?

ELLIOT

I thought that that's why you mentioned them laughing together.

KYRA

I was just trying to prove that Nadeem didn't hate gay people.

ELLIOT

Well, obviously he doesn't. *(Beat)* My kitchen window faces their yard. Whenever Brooks is out of town, I see Nadeem sneak in the back of the house for a rendezvous.

KYRA

So all those times Chaz forgot to lock the gate . . . he was actually leaving it open for Nadeem.

ELLIOT

I'm not a gossip, I swear.

KYRA

Does Brooks know?

ELLIOT

I think you might've tipped him off.

KYRA

(Nervous laughter) Oh no. That wasn't my intention at all.

ELLIOT

(Also laughs a little) I thought you did it on purpose.

KYRA

No, what kind of monster do you think I am?

ELLIOT

I wasn't sure.

(Luz reenters with Elliot's cup of tea. She clocks them laughing.)

KYRA

Do you need sugar?

LUZ

Mr. Emerson doesn't take sugar. He likes to say he's sweet enough.

ELLIOT

That's right. You don't forget anything, do you.

LUZ

Not often, no.

(Elliot sips his tea. Luz heads off.)

KYRA

So what's in the box?

ELLIOT

I've been waiting for you to ask. They're photos of the neighborhood. From back in the day. *(Opens the box and fishes through the photos)* We keep talking about history in the abstract, I thought it might be helpful for you to see up close what it is we're trying to protect.

KYRA

I already know. You don't need to convince me.

ELLIOT

Then consider this a peace offering. Now come, sit. Please.

(A moment. Kyra moves to the couch. A truce. He passes her a photo. She looks at it.)

It's the esplanade. Right out here. I'm probably four in this photo.

KYRA

Was it always this crowded?

ELLIOT

In the summer, yeah. Nobody had air conditioning, so we'd sit out under the trees to keep cool.

KYRA

People still do that.

ELLIOT

Outsiders, but yeah. No one we know. Now they sit on the grass and smoke pot, then leave their trash and go back to . . . wherever they live.

KYRA

(Beat—looks to another photo) Who's this?

ELLIOT

Oh, those are the Nettle sisters. They were music teachers. Lived in the Morrisseys' house. Everyone played an instrument back then. You'd walk through the neighborhood, and if it was spring, folks would have their windows open, and you'd hear someone at the piano, or practicing the violin. There was always music. Brahms. Mendelssohn . . .

KYRA

I still hear music on my walks.

ELLIOT

Okay, but . . . noise blasting out of a boombox isn't the same as someone sitting down to play a Bach minuet.

KYRA

Careful Elliot, your elitism is showing.

ELLIOT

Why thank you. *(Passes more photos to her)* These ones are all Haskell Ave. There used to be a barbershop up there. And this is Mr. Tesoriero. He owned the produce store. And next to him was an ice cream parlor. *Boone's*. Every day my friends and I would stop in after baseball. Mr. Boone worked behind the counter himself. But he had lost his right arm in Korea, which made scooping ice cream a little tricky. So we'd order egg creams instead. Easier to make with one arm.

KYRA

Nice kids.

ELLIOT

(A shift) Speaking of Haskell—Ruth was saying you're having trouble finding a space for your bookstore. There's a spot up there you should consider.

KYRA

A storefront?

ELLIOT

The guy who owns 860 is a friend of mine, and he's not happy with the tenant. Says they're difficult and usually late with the rent. He's looking for an excuse to nudge them out.

KYRA

Which one's 860?

ELLIOT

The wig shop. I think most of us prefer books to *wigs*. And it'd be a big step in revitalizing that strip. I could talk to the owner on your behalf.

KYRA

That's really generous of you.

ELLIOT

And if you *do* rent that spot, you're gonna want the traffic light up there. You'll see the difference it makes for the businesses.

KYRA

(Pause—gets off the couch) Okay. Now I get it. This whole time I've been trying to figure out what it is you're doing here.

ELLIOT

What do you mean?

KYRA

You butter me up with gossip, and the history of Mayberry, and then, "Oh, I know a guy with a building, I can hook you up."

ELLIOT

I'm just trying to help you.

KYRA

No, you're trying to help *yourself.* If I'm in your debt then maybe I might feel obligated to vote with you on board stuff. You scratch my / back—

ELLIOT

You're a very cynical person, you know that?

KYRA

You didn't have to do all this, Elliot. I want to protect Vernon Point the same as you. I do. I'm just not convinced it can be taken down by a stop sign. Or a paint color. Or a baluster.

ELLIOT

Well, that's where you're wrong. Those little concessions chip away at the foundation of this place. If we keep giving in, then eventually the neighborhood won't look the way it should.

KYRA

Like your photos, you mean?

ELLIOT

Someone has to hold the line.

KYRA

And that's you, I get it. You have all these wonderful memories of baseball and Bach minuets—

ELLIOT

I know you think I'm a dinosaur.

KYRA

But you can't go back in time, Elliot. Things change. You say nobody had air conditioners. But guess what? They do now.

ELLIOT

Yes, and now there's no reason to go outside and gather with the neighbors. Which, in my opinion, is a loss. I was hoping that the photos would maybe show you that.

KYRA

Yeah, the photos are nice. But also . . . kinda weird for me.

ELLIOT

Weird? Why?

KYRA

Honestly? Because everyone's *white*.

ELLIOT

(Beat) No, that's not . . .

KYRA

Look at the photos, Elliot. Everyone is white.

ELLIOT

(Flips through the photos) No, there's . . . Here's Mr. Tesoriero.

KYRA

Italians aren't white?

ELLIOT

Well, they are *now*, but . . .

KYRA

I'm not trying to make you feel guilty. I understand that that was a different time. But Elliot, you gotta know that it makes me uncomfortable, right? When you hearken back to the good old days? And rhapsodize about how much better things *used* to be?

ELLIOT

Obviously I wasn't / talking about—

KYRA

When all the neighbors looked alike and drank egg creams? I mean, that one-armed ice cream guy sounds charming, but what would've happened if it was *me* who sidled up to his counter back in the day?

ELLIOT

(Putting the photos away) Nobody's looking to go back in time. My concerns have only ever been about the architecture and landscaping / and—

KYRA

But that's not true. You also talk about *people*, and their garbage music and "outsiders" coming in to sit on our grass. And of all the storefronts up on Haskell, it's the *wig shop* you wanna help evict.

ELLIOT

The wig shop is the only store whose landlord wants to kick them out!

KYRA

I'm not gonna help displace a Black-owned business, I'm sorry.

ELLIOT

This isn't about—! Your bookstore would *also* be a Black-owned business.

KYRA

A bougier one, but yeah.

ELLIOT

I don't like what you're implying. I'll have you know that I am a lifelong *Democrat*.

KYRA

(Chuckles) Oh good.

ELLIOT

I've worked for decades to more fully integrate this neighborhood. If you want to know my *bona fides*, all you need to do is look at our board. Look at the range of people I've sold houses to.

KYRA

Yes, you've let in some of us good ones. You're a top-notch curator, I'll give you that.

ELLIOT

Alright, I think we're done.

(Luz enters as he gathers up his things.)

I came here to find a middle ground. But you clearly have no interest.

KYRA

I would *love* that actually. But I don't think it's why you came here. To find a middle ground, you'd have to cede some of the ground you've been standing on, and it doesn't seem like you're willing to do that. I think you want *all* the ground to yourself. While the rest of us have the great privilege of squatting on it.

(Elliot takes his shoebox and the enormous floral arrangement and heads for the door.)

ELLIOT

Thank you again for the flowers. If you get the receipt to Ruth, the Association can reimburse you. I'll see you at the next meeting.

KYRA

Unless you get hit by a car.

(Elliot leaves awkwardly. A little help from Luz.
After he goes, silence.)

Too far?

LUZ

No, I liked it.

KYRA

(Beat) Can you do something for me, Luz?

LUZ

What is it?

KYRA

I'd like you to tell me why you stopped working for that man.

(A moment between them. Lights out.)

SCENE 7

July Meeting
Vernon Point Neighborhood Association

Parlor. Mid-meeting. Everyone but Penny is here. A wooden baluster is being passed around. Alan takes the minutes. Luz tidies the dining room. Elliot stands at the easel with a diagram of baluster designs. People talk over each other.

ELLIOT
They had several historically accurate balusters to choose from. This is a classic Victorian. There's also French Colonial,

RUTH
Why are we still discussing balusters?

ISAAC
We should've started with the corner.

ELLIOT *(Continued)*
or a Tuscan,
which is lovely.

WILLOW
Can we please not talk over
each other?

BROOKS
I've heard no accountability
about that corner.

RUTH
After what happened to Penny,
we could get a stop sign by /
next week.

ELLIOT
I said that I could've been
more open!

ALAN
I can't write all of this down!

KYRA
Oh, you think maybe?

MELISSA
That's big of you, Elliot.

ELLIOT
(Bangs the gavel) The corner is *on* the agenda! I know emotions are high right now, but can we please plow through these last few items?

MELISSA
(Beat—heads for the dining room) I'm gonna refresh my plate. But you go on, Elliot. I can hear you.

ELLIOT
I only brought the balusters because some of you didn't seem to grasp how egregious the violation was. The one being passed around is what was originally on the porch. And *this* one is what they installed. You can see for yourselves how historically inappropriate it is. *(Hands new baluster to someone to pass around)* Now, I realize that it's never pleasant reporting a neighbor—

RUTH

A neighbor in a *wheelchair*.

ELLIOT

Be that as it may, historical preservation is part of our mandate as a board. With that, I move that we submit a violation report to Landmarks.

ISAAC

I second.

ELLIOT

All those in favor?

(Everyone raises a hand without enthusiasm.)

Approved without dissent. Next up is Security. Alan?

ALAN

Yes. I'm happy to let you know that for the first time in a while we had *zero* reports of stolen packages this month, / which—

ISAAC

I think I know why that / might be.

ALAN

I'm not *finished*! *(Silence)* As I was saying, we had zero reports of stolen packages this month, which is a big relief. And now . . . Isaac, you may have the floor.

ISAAC

Thank you. I just wanted to add that I had a nice chat with the two young porch pirates—Carter and Devon. I showed them our security footage, and they promised to cut the shit.

KYRA

Well done.

ISAAC

As a bonus, Brooks, they handed over your son's bike. It's in my garage whenever you want to pick it up. Hopefully your husband can be more vigilant about the back gate.

BROOKS

Oh, he and I had a chat, and that back gate won't be left open again.

ISAAC

Also, I hired the porch boys to work with my crew on the weekends.

WILLOW	ALAN	KYRA
That's really nice, Isaac.	You hired them?	Wow, that's amazing.

ISAAC

Hopefully I can keep them out of trouble.

RUTH

Hopefully they don't steal your truck.

ELLIOT

And on that cheerful note, we're at Traffic and Safety. You're all obviously champing at the bit, so let's discuss. Kyra?

KYRA

Thanks. But I don't think there's much to discuss anymore. It's clear we need stop signs at the corner. But if anyone disagrees, please speak up. *(Looks to Elliot, he says nothing)* Great. Because I'd actually like to pivot to the light installed on Haskell—which caused all the problems in the first place.

ELLIOT

What's the point in that? If the consensus is to apply for stop signs, what difference does the light on Haskell make?

KYRA

I'm glad you asked, because the answer is pretty interesting.

(Melissa returns with food. Luz sets the street diagram on the easel. Then she retreats, but doesn't leave the room.)

ISAAC

Yes, more easel.

KYRA

Last meeting, I suggested getting rid of the Haskell light since it was diverting drivers onto Palmer, but Elliot didn't like that idea.

ELLIOT

No, I just said that the city probably had a reason to install it.

KYRA

And you were right. I called a few city offices looking into the situation, and I discovered that the light was put in at the request of HAMBA, the Haskell Ave. Merchant and Business Association.

BROOKS

But . . . don't you sit on that board, Elliot?

ELLIOT

I do. That's hardly a secret.

KYRA

And yet, in all our talk about that light, you never mentioned your role in getting it installed.

ELLIOT

Because I didn't *have* a role.

KYRA

That's so strange, because when I asked Nadeem, who also sits on that board, he said that you were the one who *initiated* that light.

MELISSA

Is that true?

ELLIOT

Okay, putting aside Nadeem's blatant breach of HAMBA confidentiality, that light was installed because *many* business owners *collectively* felt that the traffic situation on Haskell was untenable. You all know what it was like up there—dangerous to cross, impossible to turn—

KYRA

And really hard to get to your office.

ELLIOT

Hold on—

RUTH

It's true. You've complained for years that your clients couldn't turn into your lot without circling the block.

KYRA

(Indicates on the diagram) And conveniently the new light was put in here—right by your office—so now pulling into the lot is a piece of cake.

ELLIOT

Okay, you're obviously trying to have some kind of *Perry Mason* moment here, but that light helped *everyone* on that strip, not just me.

KYRA

Unfortunately, it also impacted the lives of your Vernon Point neighbors in a deeply negative way, which is kinda the *opposite* of what you're supposed to be doing on this board. All the accidents on this corner, and you never once copped to being the *cause* of them.

ELLIOT

Jesus, I wasn't the *cause* of / anything.

KYRA

Even after Penny was hit, you *still* / didn't— [speak up.]

ELLIOT

You can't blame me for Penny! It was raining, and she was rushing and not looking when she crossed!

ALAN

She didn't have a *chance* to look. That car came flying down Palmer with no reason to stop.

KYRA

Bottom line? You do some shady shit, and it hurts the neighborhood.

ELLIOT

I don't hurt th—! I *protect* this neighborhood!

KYRA

While acting in your own self-interest.

ELLIOT

This is absurd. I don't want any of this in the minutes! *(Back to Kyra)* If you don't like how this board is run, you're welcome to step down.

MELISSA	ISAAC	BROOKS
Why should *she* step down?	Okay, take it easy.	I saw *that* coming.

KYRA

I'm sorry, Elliot, but you treat these thirty square blocks as your personal fiefdom. You decide what happens, what's / appropriate—

ELLIOT

Nothing happens without the board's approval!

RUTH

But as president you *do* hold tremendous sway.

KYRA

And as the primary realtor, you pretty much decide who gets to *live* here.

ELLIOT

No, I don't control who people sell their homes to! I'm not a *gatekeeper*!

KYRA

Yes, you are! That's *exactly* what you are. Look at Luz!

(Beat. Everyone looks to Luz. She's confused.)

Tell them what you told me. Tell them why you quit working for Elliot.

BROOKS

Okay, here we go.

LUZ

I told you that in confidence.

MELISSA

Is it something we should know?

ELLIOT

(To Kyra) What are you doing?

KYRA

If you don't want to share, obviously you don't have to.

ELLIOT

I'm sorry, but Luz is not on the board. She has no business speaking.

LUZ

(Looks to him, stung) I have no business *speaking*?

ELLIOT

You're not even a resident of Vernon Point.

LUZ

I've worked in these houses for *thirty* years.

ELLIOT

That doesn't mean you *live* here.

LUZ

I've made your meals, changed your sheets, / bathed your children.

ELLIOT

(Bangs the gavel) This is not appropriate. There are *rules* that must / be followed.

ISAAC

I move to let Luz address the board.

BROOKS

I second.

MELISSA

All those in favor?

ELLIOT

I am running this meeting!

(Everyone but Elliot has raised a hand.)

MELISSA

The ayes have it. Go on, Luz.

LUZ

(Beat, steps closer) For those who don't know, I live on the other side of Haskell. It's not far but . . . it's very different. My building isn't as bad as some of them, but it *is* too crowded, and too noisy. Would I rather have lived here? Of course. Who wouldn't? I know that my *son* did.

ELLIOT

What *is* this?

LUZ

Felix used to come to work with me on weekends. Mr. Emerson, you and Mrs. Emerson were always very kind to him. He'd read on the porch and you'd talk to him; you taught him to play chess; he became friends with your sons.

RUTH

And my daughters.

LUZ

We always felt like we belonged here. Even if we didn't *live* here. *(Beat)* Still, in my heart I knew this would only ever be a place where I worked. But *Felix* thought otherwise. He was a good student. And after college he got a good job with a good salary. A *very* good salary, actually. And last year he took me out for my birthday, he and his wife and their new baby.

RUTH

(To those who don't know) His name is Rocket.

LUZ

And at dinner Felix said, "Nanay, Dr. Klein's house is for sale. I want to buy it, and I want us all to live there together."

(A moment as the others process this.)

MELISSA

Dr. Klein's house?

BROOKS

This house? Felix wanted to buy *this* house?

LUZ

When it was on the market, yes. He had enough money, and Mr. Emerson was the realtor. So Felix put in the offer. But then Mr. Emerson came back and said that someone else came in above asking.

KYRA

We obviously didn't know who we were bidding against.

LUZ

Felix wanted to negotiate, but Mr. Emerson said that the sale was already done.

ELLIOT

Which is what can happen sometimes.

LUZ

So you said. *(To the others)* But many months later, when I was still at the Emersons', they had some friends over. They were all in the front parlor, and it was late, so I said my goodbyes. But halfway home I realized that I had forgotten my phone, so I went back. Only no one heard me come in. I was just gonna run in and out, but I heard them talking in the next room. A little loud from the cocktails. And Ken Horace said something about Dr. Klein.

ELLIOT

Luz, you don't have to— [do this.]

LUZ

And I heard Mr. Emerson say, "Did you know that my Luz and her son tried to buy his house?" And Mr. Horace said, "No, what happened?" And Mr. Emerson said, "Oh, I nipped that right in the bud. There's no way I'm gonna let my maid live in a bigger house than me."

(Silence.)

ELLIOT

That's not exactly what / was said.

LUZ

That is *word. For. Word. (To the others)* I was so taken aback that I dropped my phone, and they got quiet in the next room.

Then Mrs. Emerson called out, "Luz? Is that you?" So I said, "Yes, I just forgot something," and I fled. The next day I gave my notice.

BROOKS

(Beat) Wow, that's a really shitty story.

ISAAC

I'm sorry, Luz.

MELISSA

Thank you for sharing that.

(Luz steps back but doesn't leave.)

ELLIOT

Look, sometimes you have a few drinks and say things you don't mean.

KYRA

So you *didn't* torpedo Felix buying the house?

ELLIOT

I'm not gonna argue every point here. My job as a realtor is to serve my client. I did that. I don't see what any of this has to do with the *board*.

KYRA

It gets to your integrity and whether you should be in charge.

ELLIOT

What is *that* supposed to mean?

MELISSA

She's right. The bylaws have a pretty clear code of ethics when it comes to honesty, transparency, conflicts of interest—

ELLIOT

Okay, this is ludicrous.

MELISSA

But it's not. Installing that light helped your business. Board members are obligated to disclose personal interests that compromise our duties to the community. You didn't do that.

ELLIOT

(Turns on Kyra) I tried to work with you! I offered you an olive branch!

KYRA

By bringing me photos? A box of dead people that no one remembers?

ELLIOT

I remember them! *Someone* should! And we're not all dead by the way!

KYRA

Not yet maybe, but soon from what I hear.

(A moment. Most of them aren't sure what to make of this. Kyra regrets saying it.)

Sorry, that was— [too far.]

ELLIOT

(Looks to Isaac) Did you say something to her?

ISAAC

I just mentioned that you were back in treatment, that's all. You've been dealing with a lot, and I was trying to get her to hang back.

ELLIOT

And do what? Run down the clock? So you all could do what you wanted after I was gone?

RUTH

I'm confused. Are you actually sick again?

ELLIOT

It doesn't matter. Because I'm not going anywhere. You wanna wait me out? Then settle in, because I'm staying right where I am.

KYRA

Or maybe you're not. I make a motion to remove Elliot as president.

(Silence.)

ELLIOT

You want to remove me? Who the fuck do you think you are?

WILLOW

Okay, let's all take a deep breath.

ELLIOT

You want to *remove* me, Kyra?

KYRA

Given everything that's happened, yes, it's the right thing to do.

ELLIOT

You *can't* remove me. Check the bylaws. Every household gets a vote. You need to poll the entire Association to remove me.

MELISSA

From the board, yes. But not from your *office*. We can remove an officer by simple board majority. According to the bylaws.

ELLIOT

(Beat) Is this why you wanted Kyra on the board? To give you leverage?

MELISSA

What are you talking about?

ELLIOT

Don't play dumb, Melissa. You've had your eye on my gavel for years!

ISAAC

You're being paranoid, Elliot.

MELISSA

As vice president, it falls on me to conduct the vote.

ELLIOT

You're awful familiar with these bylaws. But I'm *paranoid*. Okay.

MELISSA

Kyra has moved to hold a vote—

BROOKS

I second.

MELISSA

Thank you. Elliot, as the officer in question you obviously aren't allowed to cast a vote. Sorry about that. But everyone else . . .

RUTH

Can I just say something? Because I've known Elliot longer than any of you. And yes, he's always been an ass.

ELLIOT

Okay—

RUTH

You know it's true. And Kyra's right, you can be a bully, and dishonest, and we would've been *lucky* to have Felix and his family as neighbors.

ELLIOT

Can we just cut to / the vote?

RUTH

At the same time, no one has worked harder for Vernon Point. It was Elliot who fought to get this place landmarked. It wouldn't exist without him.

KYRA

How is that relevant?

RUTH

You said you chose Vernon Point because it was nice. You liked the trees and the bikes and how old-timey it all felt. Everything that attracted you to this place is a direct result of Elliot's work.

KYRA

Good work doesn't excuse bad behavior.

RUTH

I agree. That's why this is hard. I hate what Elliot did. But I can't ignore that he's also a friend. He sold us our house. He and Gracie babysat our kids. He was at my Lizzy's wedding.

ELLIOT

Weddings, actually.

RUTH

Yes. And when my Ezra passed, Elliot brought me groceries and shoveled my driveway, and I'm not the only one he's done that for. I know what a good person he is. And what an awful person he can sometimes be. Just like most everyone I know. People are messy.

BROOKS

Yeah, but there's messy and then there's *messy*.

RUTH

I get it. But also . . . come on, the guy has / *cancer*.

ELLIOT

Please don't bring that into / this, Ruth.

KYRA

I'm sorry, but that can't be a get-out-of-jail-free card.

RUTH

Of course not. But maybe this is a chance to show Elliot the kind of grace that he hasn't always shown others, and remind him what community actually means. Not by erasing consequences, but by refusing to discard people when they fail us.

(It's hard to tell if her plea has moved anyone.)

MELISSA

With that, we should vote.

ELLIOT

Is this what you wanted, Luz?

LUZ

I was just hoping for the stop signs.

MELISSA

All those in favor of removing Elliot as president of the board?

(A moment. Kyra raises her hand. Then Brooks. Then Melissa. No one else raises a hand.)

KYRA

Are you kidding me?

ALAN

I know that what he said was bad. And I kinda feel like what happened to Penny was maybe his fault. But . . .

KYRA

But that's not *enough* for you.

ELLIOT

All those opposed? *(To Melissa)* Sorry. You do it.

MELISSA

(Without enthusiasm) All those opposed?

(Alan, Ruth and eventually Isaac raise their hands. Everyone looks to Willow.)

WILLOW

Sorry. This is really hard. Because . . .

BROOKS

Because you can't vote against your uncle?

WILLOW

He's not my uncle!

MELISSA

Then you vote to keep him?

WILLOW

No, I can't do that either. I'm sorry, Elliot. But . . . I abstain.

RUTH

Jesus. Even her votes are nonbinary.

ELLIOT

It doesn't matter. It takes a majority to vote me out. A tie isn't a majority. Sorry, Kyra. Attempted coup rebuffed.

(The doorbell rings. Luz hurries to answer it.)

For future reference, wishful thinking is not a voting strategy.

(Luz has let in Penny, who walks with a cane and is wearing a neck brace.)

PENNY

Hello, Luz. Hello, everyone.

RUTH	ALAN	ISAAC	BROOKS
Well look who made it.	There she is!	She's back in business!	Hey, beautiful!

(Alan helps Penny into the parlor and to her usual seat over the following.)

KYRA

Penny wasn't up to a full meeting but wanted to catch the tail end. *(To Penny)* Cutting it kinda close.

PENNY

Yeah, well, I'm not as nimble as I was a few weeks ago. *(To the others)* I wanted to thank you all for the get-well flowers. They were beautiful.

MELISSA

How are you feeling?

PENNY

Better every day. How about you?

MELISSA

I'm fine.

PENNY

Oh good. And Bailey?

MELISSA

(Beat) Bailey's great. Thanks for asking.

PENNY

(Settled in now) Did I miss the vote?

ELLIOT

How do you know about the vote?

KYRA

I might've given her a heads-up.

ELLIOT

(Beat) And you say you're not cunning. What a load of horseshit.

MELISSA

We were just doing the tally. It's three to three with one abstention.

PENNY

Oo, a nail-biter! It's a good thing I showed up. *(To Elliot)* Don't worry, I won't stretch this out. Elliot, you're one of my dearest friends, and I know how much your work as president means to you. But I think it's time to let someone else lead the charge.

ELLIOT

Don't do this, / Penny.

PENNY

I vote in favor of Elliot's removal.

(Silence as the weight of this settles in.)

MELISSA

Thank you. With the majority of votes, the ayes have it.

PENNY

I wish you had just said yes to the stop signs. We'd both be better off.

ELLIOT

(Simmering) What a bunch of hypocrites. You were there that night of the Luz thing, Ruth, same as me. So was Alan. And Penny. Willow. You were all there.

BROOKS

(News to him) I guess my invitation was lost in the mail.

ELLIOT

(To Luz) Why didn't you mention any of *them*?

LUZ

Because they didn't say what you said.

ELLIOT

Still, they *laughed* when I said it.

RUTH	WILLOW
No, hold on a second.	Not everyone, Elliot.

ELLIOT

But I'm the one being punished. Because of a joke.

KYRA

But it wasn't a joke. And it's not the only reason.

ELLIOT

(Turns on her) I should never have let you in here.

(Unable to contain his fury, Elliot grabs the historical, Revival baluster and swings it like a bat, smashing the diagram and easel. It's instant chaos as the others scramble away.)

MELISSA	ISAAC	WILLOW
Jesus Christ!	Alright, calm down!	Oh my god!

BROOKS	RUTH	KYRA
The fuck?	Stop it, Elliot!	What are you *doing*, Elliot?!

(Elliot raises the baluster as if contemplating who to smash with it first. He runs upstage of the couch.)

ISAAC	BROOKS	KYRA
Elliot, no!	Hey! Hey!	Stop it!

ALAN	PENNY	RUTH
Where are you going?	What in the world?	Oh for godsakes.

(Elliot scans the room for options, then runs to a nearby vase of flowers, smashing it into a wall and sending the flowers flying everywhere.)

ISAAC	RUTH	MELISSA
Heads!	What are you *doing*?!	Penny, watch out!

KYRA	WILLOW	ALAN
Stop it, Elliot!	Alan, block her!	He's gonna hurt someone!

(In the mayhem, board members take cover. Or race to help. Alan tries to shield Penny from the flying debris. Luz tries to catch things before they fall so she doesn't have to clean them up later. Elliot looks to the dining room, then runs for it as Kyra realizes what's about to happen.)

KYRA

No! Not the china! NOT THE CHINA!

(But it's too late. Elliot swings the baluster, smashing the cheese plate, the fruit bowl, the wine glasses and, yes, the china—lots of it broken to bits. Kyra rushes to stop Elliot.)

RUTH	MELISSA	WILLOW
Someone grab him!	Kyra, be careful!	Watch out!

ALAN	BROOKS	LUZ
Oh god.	Hey!	Careful of the—!

(Eventually Kyra tries to wrestle the baluster from Elliot's grip. As they struggle, they move back into the parlor. Isaac and Brooks try to break it up.)

ALAN	RUTH	KYRA
Now what?	Get in there!	Let go!
ISAAC	BROOKS	WILLOW
Enough, Elliot!	Put the baluster down!	This isn't you, Elliot!

(Kyra gets the baluster. Isaac and Brooks pull them apart. Kyra charges at Elliot, the baluster in hand, but Isaac gets it away from her.)

KYRA

Are you out of your mind?!

ELLIOT

I'm sorry!

KYRA

What if my girls were here?!

ELLIOT

I'm sorry! I shouldn't have lost my temper!

KYRA

You need to get out of my house.

ELLIOT

I'll pay for everything I broke.

KYRA

Elliot please, go before I do something historically inappropriate!

(A moment. Elliot stands and starts to pack up his things over the following.)

ELLIOT

I'm sorry, but the neighborhood is important to me.

BROOKS

Just stop.

ELLIOT

It's special, and it's disappearing, and no one seems to care.

ISAAC

You need to go, buddy.

ELLIOT

Every day something new slips away. Wonderful things. To me at least. Why would we let them go? That's all I was trying to say.

ISAAC

(Gently now) Okay.

ELLIOT

I'm the one who remembers. That's my job. And if I'm not here . . . who will remember?

RUTH

I'll remember, Elliot.

ELLIOT

(Unable to hold back the emotion) There are so many good things, right in front of us. And we should hold on to them. As tight as we can for as long as we can. Because it's all going so quickly. Don't you see that? It's going too quickly.

(Silence. Elliot is about to head out when . . .)

MELISSA

Elliot. I'm sorry. *(He stops to face her)* I'm gonna need the gavel.

(A moment. He reluctantly pulls the gavel from his bag and holds it out to her. She takes it.

Then he heads into the foyer, where Luz opens the door for him.)

ELLIOT

Please apologize to Felix for me.

(A beat. Elliot leaves.

No one says anything for a few moments. The calm after the storm.)

RUTH

I just want to go on the record. I did *not* laugh that night, Luz. I thought that what Elliot said was shameful.

KYRA

Did you tell him that? When he said it?

RUTH

(Beat) No, you're right, I should've said something.

ALAN

We all should've.

KYRA

It's fascinating. I mean, I'm not surprised, but . . . it's fascinating.

PENNY

What is?

KYRA

Just . . . how you all are when we're not in the room.

WILLOW

Well, we don't place bets on you, if that's what you mean.

(Luz heads to the dining room to clean up. Others may straighten up over the following.)

ISAAC

Elliot was right though. You are kinda hypocrites.

RUTH

I think he meant *all* of us, Isaac. Not just—

ISAAC

I'm not a hypocrite. You all know me. What you see is what you get.

RUTH

Right. Upstanding, salt of the earth, self-made man. Renovated houses until he could buy one of his own.

ISAAC

Exactly.

RUTH

Except you leave out the part where your crew is overworked and underpaid. Which is how you could afford that house.

ISAAC

That is *bullshit*.

ALAN

I've heard the same thing.

ISAAC

My wife is a *doctor*, I don't need to take advantage of my crew.

RUTH

Which makes it worse. You don't need to, but you do it anyway.

BROOKS

Well done. But now I'm curious. How am *I* a hypocrite, Ruth?

MELISSA

Let's not do this. Everyone's upset / and—

RUTH

Easy. Culturally sensitive travel writer reduces local shop owner to Muslim stereotype.

BROOKS

That's not at all what I did. And you can't really compare *that* to Elliot.

RUTH

You asked me a question and I answered it.

BROOKS

You realize that's the definition of false equivalency, right?

ALAN

Now do Willow.

WILLOW

Nobody needs to do / Willow.

PENNY

I can do Willow. She says she's vegan but every meeting I see her sneaking pork dumplings.

WILLOW

That's not hypocrisy, it's a relapse!

PENNY

See that? You all think I've lost a step, but I see *everything*.

RUTH

Except oncoming cars.

PENNY

(Chuckles) You bitch.

KYRA

Okay, but Elliot isn't a dumpling.

BROOKS

Thank you.

ISAAC

This is fun. Now someone do Kyra.

MELISSA

No, Kyra's been through enough. Let's just wrap this up.

LUZ

I can do Kyra.

(Silence. Luz steps back into the room.)

KYRA

I know, I shouldn't have asked you to tell that Elliot story. That wasn't fair to you. I'm sorry.

LUZ

Thanks. But that's not the one I'm thinking of.

PENNY

Oo! What's the one you're thinking of?

LUZ

It's about the bookstore she wants to open.

KYRA

(Beat) What about it?

LUZ

You told Elliot that you'd never displace a Black-owned business. But I heard you call the owner of the building yesterday and ask if the space with the wig shop might be available.

KYRA

(Beat) They were getting kicked out whether I took the space or not.

LUZ

Right. *(Then)* You've been so worried about fitting in. Well congrats, you did it.

(Luz moves to clean something up.)

ALAN

Let me help you clean up, Luz.

LUZ

(Stops) Thank you, but I think I'm done. My son's right, I don't actually *need* to do this. You all can clean up after yourselves now.

(Luz heads off, grabs her stuff from the coat closet, then exits through the front door.)

RUTH

Are we finished? Because I'd like to go home.

WILLOW

I can stay and help pick up.

ALAN

Same.

BROOKS

(To Kyra) You good?

KYRA

I'll be fine. *(Beat)* But next month, maybe someone else can host.

MELISSA

And with that, I call this meeting adjourned.

(Melissa bangs the gavel. Lights out.)

END OF PLAY

JOAN MARCUS

DAVID LINDSAY-ABAIRE is a Tony- and Pulitzer Prize–winning playwright, screenwriter, lyricist, and librettist. His most recent show, the musical *Kimberly Akimbo*, written with composer Jeanine Tesori, premiered off Broadway, where it won the Lortel, NYDCC, OCC, and Drama Desk Awards for Best Musical. After its move to Broadway, the show won five Tony Awards, including Best Musical, Best Book, and Best Score, and garnered a Grammy nomination for Best Musical Theater Album. His play *Good People* premiered on Broadway and was awarded the New York Drama Critics Circle Award for Best Play, the Horton Foote Prize, the Edgerton Foundation New American Play Award, and two Tony nominations. His play *Rabbit Hole* also premiered on Broadway and received the Pulitzer Prize for Drama, five Tony nominations, and the Spirit of America Award. David also wrote the book and lyrics for *Shrek the Musical* (music by Jeanine Tesori), which was nominated for eight Tonys, four Oliviers, and a Grammy and earned David the Kleban Prize as America's most promising musical theatre lyricist. David's other works include the book to the musical *High Fidelity* (music by Tom Kitt, lyrics by Amanda Green) and his plays *Ripcord*, *Fuddy Meers*, *Kimberly Akimbo*, *Wonder of the World*, and *A Devil Inside*, among others. In addition to his work in theatre, David's screen credits include his film adaptation of *Rabbit Hole* (starring Nicole Kidman, Oscar nomination), *Rise of the Guardians*, *Poltergeist*, *Oz the Great and Powerful*, *Robots*, *Inkheart*, and *The Family Fang*, among others. He is also, along with Tanya Barfield, codirector of the Lila Acheson Wallace American Playwrights Program at the Juilliard School.